The Biggest Disability
Is a Bad Attitude

Why They Call Me
"the Confidence Coach"
and How I Can Help You

Scott Ballard

Confidence Coach LLC
Hillsboro, OR

For more information contact:
Confidence Coach LLC
22115 NW Imbrie Dr., Ste. 340
Hillsboro, OR 97124
1-800-768-2217

ISBN: 978-0-692-37717-8 – paperback
ISBN: 978-0-692-37716-1 – eBook

Library of Congress Control Number:
2015935053

Why the different font?

You'll notice that there is a different font being used throughout *The Biggest Disability is a Bad Attitude*. It may be one you're not normally used to seeing, but it serves a very special purpose. In addition to making my book stand out, it also makes the book readable for all people with different kinds of reading abilities. This allows me to reach a wider audience, so as you read, keep this in mind!

CONTENTS

CHAPTER ONE

Your Job Is to Change the World; My Job Is Never to Let You Forget That

I want to begin this book by telling you something that I know from the bottom of my heart to be absolutely true: You are a person who can change the world. I believe that you can go out every day and do things that only you can do. You can use your God-given ability every day to truly make a difference.

I know how hard it can be to believe this. I know that the challenges you face may seem insurmountable. I know because I've been through it all myself.

My story begins in the first grade. Up until that point, I was a happy child. I loved my parents and siblings, and they loved me. All my memories are like beautiful dreams. I was incredibly excited to start school with all my friends, and I was ready to love school as much as I loved everything else in my life.

A couple of months into the school year, however, I started to notice that something wasn't right. Everyone around me was learning to read and write, but to me, it didn't make any sense. Everything was difficult. Words seemed jumbled up, seemed not to have meaning, and I couldn't make any sense of them. I became increasingly discouraged.

Back in the sixties, when I was in grade school, the practice in small towns like the one I grew up in was for the teacher to come over to your house and have dinner with your family at the beginning of every school year. They would tell your parents how you were doing, and how things were going so far.

When my teacher showed up and had her conversation with my parents, she explained that I was having trouble in class. She told my parents that I needed to focus more, to try harder. So my parents, who were strict, told me that I needed to buckle down. Being a very compliant child, I agreed.

I buckled down. I worked hard. But things did not get any better, and by the end of the year it had become very clear to me that I did not have the same facility for learning as my classmates. In the sixties, there were no programs or arrangements for dealing with somebody like me— somebody with dyslexia— so I was basically pushed to the side and left to flounder.

It was a miserable year. Other students made fun of me. I was told I was stupid. I was put in a corner by the teacher and essentially called a dunce. I was mocked during recess. It was the most wretched experience a first-grader could have. I dreaded going to school every morning. Then, at the end of this terrible year, the teacher came back to my house for another meeting with my parents, and made a horrifying recommendation: I should be held back. I was going to have to repeat the first grade.

Despite my academic troubles, I was a very social young boy who had a lot of friends. My first thought when I heard this horrible news was that all my friends were going to move on and I was going to have to stay behind. It was the most embarrassing thing that had happened in my life.

That summer was the longest summer in the history of the world. I was so mortified that I didn't tell any of my friends what had happened, that I wouldn't be in second grade with them. I was incredibly depressed and discouraged— and I was angry.

My second time through first grade was even worse than the first. I started running away from school. I acted out. I became like a lightning rod. Despite being a year older than my classmates, I was one of the smallest kids in the class, but when the other kids would pick on me I would immediately get into a fight. I started to seriously wonder whether this life was really worth living. I lived in a rural area and had plenty of access to knives, guns, and axes. I came very close to saying, "This is not worth it. I don't want to continue on." It was an incredibly dark time for me. Today, at age fifty-five, I can still feel the horror of that darkness.

Throughout this, my parents and family remained incredibly loving and supportive. But there were simply no real solutions. So my family prayed. Then one day, as my mom was praying, one of the ladies in her prayer group spoke up. She told my mom that she had a dyslexic son, and had trained at a university in New York so that she could teach him how to read and write. And she could do the same for me.

God had answered my family's prayers and sent to our tiny rural Oregon town of ten thousand a trained professional from New York City who would be able to help me learn to read and write. The miracle had begun.

This woman, whose husband was the pastor of the Methodist church in town, began to tutor me, and began to show me that God loved me. I began to truly believe that God had a plan and a purpose for me, that he loved me, that I wasn't alone, and that I wasn't garbage.

I can't begin to put into words what an impact this experience had on me—an impact that still resonates today. It made me the person I am. To realize, as an eight-year-old boy, that God cared enough about me to send someone from New York to this small, rural town to care for me, to help me—it changed my life to know that love and acceptance.

For the next four years, day in and day out, she tutored me. My parents didn't have very much money, so in exchange for the tutoring my mother cleaned my tutor's house, did her laundry, and took care of her chores. In return, I would meet with the tutor in the morning before I went to school, and at recess and lunch I would go off to a separate room to continue working with her. Mom, I just want to say thank you from the bottom of my heart for your loving sacrifice. You're my hero.

After a couple of years of this regime, another miracle happened. I was riding in the car with my mother, and we pulled up to an intersection and came to a stop. I looked out the window, I looked at the sign— *and I could read it.* I could actually read it! It may sound like the smallest thing in the world, but being able to look at that sign and read the word "stop" was a true miracle.

From that point on I was like a kid with the greatest toy in the world. I drove everybody crazy because every sign, every billboard, every set of directions I could see, I would read. I butchered most of them, but I was starting to be able to put them together. To me, it was like magic.

Despite this success, I still struggled in school. The teachers, not knowing what to do with me, just passed me by. Because I couldn't excel academically, I instead became very helpful, kind, and considerate. I was never a problem in school. Then, when I reached sixth grade, I had the privilege of being taught by one of the most extraordinary, out-of-the-box teachers you could possibly imagine in the sixties. Through my experience in his class—an experience I will discuss in more detail in a later chapter—I learned that God had given me the ability to understand business in a way that none of the other kids could seem to understand. I began to truly find my place in the world.

When I finally graduated, nobody was more surprised than I was. My GPA was somewhere around 2.5, but somehow I still managed to receive my diploma. I think the school administrators appreciated that I was always on time, that I was never a problem, and that I always tried my hardest.

Most important, I learned that while academics were not going to be my future, there was a path for me. My

sixth-grade experience taught me
that I could be a leader. I was a good
risk taker, and I learned a lot by
failing. Being responsible and taking a
leadership role came naturally to me.
I was very good at delegating, and at
empowering the other kids to do their
best. And I realized that this was
my God-given ability. I wasn't good
at reading and I was even worse at
writing and math, but I could inspire
and encourage and empower people to
be their best selves.

And the truth is, this God-given
ability came directly out of my so-
called disability. We as a society
have misinterpreted what we view
as disabilities, disadvantages, or
roadblocks. I have discovered that
for most people, their "roadblock" is
actually their greatest advantage.

When I started my own company,
my disability prevented my ego
from convincing me that I could

do everything. Instead, one of my greatest gifts to the company was my ability to find people and empower them. I would find someone who was very good at selling, and I would believe in them and give them full responsibility. By doing this, I was able to build a team of people who could do what they were passionate about and what they were best at. Thanks to this teambuilding, our insurance brokerage company was able to grow from a kitchen-table operation into a company that covered forty-two states.

Seeing this success, people asked me where I went to school, what degrees I had. "I barely got out of high school!" I told them. When they asked how I'd accomplished what I had with the company, I told them that I'd done it by surrounding myself with people smarter than me, who were geniuses in their own areas. What I did was to provide leadership and a vision of where we could go, and a belief that each and every person could truly make a difference.

That is how I change the world: by helping you understand that what you consider your disability may actually be your greatest ability. It may actually be your ability to change the world. We can't change the world from our weakness. If we try to change the world from our weakness, all we will do is struggle, fail, and become discouraged and depressed. Instead, we need to find our strength, our God-given ability. Each and every person has a God-given ability to change the world. My ability is to help other people find their own abilities. I want to challenge you and hold you accountable for reaching your God-given potential on a daily basis.

Sometimes it can be hard to see the path to your own God-given ability. It can be hard when everybody around you is telling you that there is only one path to follow, only one way to make a difference, and you know it's a path on which you can't succeed. I almost got swallowed up by that dark mindset. I almost got caught in the trap of what I call the **GREAT ACADEMIC LIE.** In our culture, we send our children into the school system, and whether you are square or round, you are forced to fit into a certain shaped hole. And when you get to be a junior or a senior, only one path is discussed: going to college. If you don't fit that model, you are told that you are going to be a janitor.

However, for kids like me—and for the 25–30 percent of kids who have a learning disability—that path may not be the most viable option. Even with the amazing resources and tools that now exist to assist children with learning difficulty, continuing on to a college or university just doesn't make sense for some of us. And far too many of those kids are told that there is no other path.

I am here to tell you that there is another path. You can follow the path of your own God-given ability, and you can change the world. No matter how many people tell you that you can't do it, I know that you can. In fact, I actually miss all those people who told me that I would never make it, who called me stupid, who said that I would never amount to anything. They were the fuel to my fire. Every day I would listen to them and think, *I will turn myself inside out to prove to you that I am not just a stupid kid sitting in a corner, a kid nobody wants to bother with. I am going to make a difference. I am going to change the world.*

I am living proof that each of you, no matter what disability you may be facing, can find your own way to change the world. All you need to do is believe in yourself—and all I need to do is to help you keep believing.

CHAPTER TWO

We Know What You Don't Have, But What Do You Have That You're Grateful For?

When I look back and take inventory of my life, and of the processes that allowed me to overcome my disability, there is one thing that truly changed my whole perspective and way of living: **GRATITUDE.**

Instead of looking at what I didn't have and what hadn't happened, instead of thinking about what someone else had that I didn't, instead of focusing on my problems and my struggles and my disability, I started to take account and keep score of all the things I had and all the things I was grateful for. I started to make gratitude one of the main pillars of my life. And this has completely changed my thinking about who I am and why I am the way I am.

My parents taught my siblings and me that while people can do whatever they want to you— treat you in whatever way they want, say whatever they want to you— **one thing people can never do is take away your choice in how you respond. They can never take away how you choose to think about yourself.**

You always have the choice. You are always in control. You can always consider, *How am I going to react to this? How am I going to process this? How am I going to think about this? How am I going to respond?* That's what it all comes down to: **MAKING A CHOICE.**

One of the choices I made at a very young age, I made almost subconsciously. Because I had so many things negatively affecting my life, because people were telling me negative things about myself so often, I decided to think about everything in my life that I was grateful for. Every night before I went to sleep, I sat in my little bunk bed and thought, I'm really grateful for my grandmother and how much she loves me. *I'm really grateful for how much my parents care about me. I'm really grateful for my two best friends who live across the street. I'm really grateful that today I got to play football.*

This may sound trivial. It may sound like a little kid thinking about little things. But it's that kind of thinking that has made me the positive, encouraging person I am today. In fact, that's the number-one thing people say about me: that I am one of the most positive, encouraging people they've ever met.

The reason for that is simple: **GRATITUDE**. I've made a practice in my life of being grateful. Gratitude has allowed me to be able to serve people without any expectation of them ever being able to do anything for me. Instead, I am simply grateful for the opportunity, for how good it makes me feel in my heart and soul.

We wonder why we are so discontented and unhappy and stressed; why we have so much anxiety. The answer is simple: we spend too much time thinking about what we don't have instead of what we do have. Gratitude is like an inoculation against being discouraged, upset, afraid, or depressed. We all have those low times, but gratitude can help us find our way out of them.

When I am feeling down in some way, I stop and consider all the things I am grateful for, and to whom I am grateful. When I focus on those things, I start to appreciate them more, and they become more valuable to me. I think about God, my wife and kids, friends, clients, experiences, places, etc., and realize that I am amazingly blessed.

You can live a different life, with a different purpose, and a different intention. Start leading a life of gratitude. Take into account— on a daily basis— everything you are grateful for. What are you grateful for that happened today?

I have a six-month process that I go through with my Confidence Coach clients, and the entire process starts with the gratitude habit; the simple task of tallying the things you are grateful for in your life today.

So I am going to ask you to do what I ask my clients to do at the beginning of our session:

Write down three things that you are grateful for right now.

1. _____

2. _____

3. _____

Write down three things that you are grateful for from yesterday.

1. _____

2. _____

3. _____

Write down three things that you are grateful for from last week.

1. _____

2. _____

3. _____

Now write down why you are grateful for each of those things.

_____

_____

_____

_____

_____

_____

_____

_____

_____

_____

_____

_____

_____

_____

_____

_____

And finally, write down why each of these things is important to you.

_____

_____

_____

_____

_____

_____

_____

_____

_____

_____

_____

_____

_____

_____

_____

_____

_____

The next thing I'm going to ask you to do is go all the way back to your first memories of childhood. Write down all the things you were grateful for then, and that you are grateful for now. It doesn't matter how big or small—write it all down.

_____

_____

_____

_____

_____

_____

_____

_____

_____

_____

_____

_____

_____

And then keep going. Create your own personal story of gratitude, of all the things you have been grateful for throughout your life. Write down your life of gratitude. And when you are finished, take that story and share it with your family and friends.

I call this tool The Gratitude Experience™. At Confidence Coach, we have just finished developing our first e-learning course, which is focused on this daily habit of being grateful. The course starts with today, and it goes all the way back to your first memories as a child using steps like the ones above. At the end of the course, you make a gratitude statement for your life and share it with your family and friends. This can help you become a grateful person— which in turn can help you change the world.

Sometimes, when I ask people to do this exercise, they simply can't. They cannot think of three things that they are grateful for. "This is stupid," they say. "I can't do this. It doesn't make sense." The culture we live in doesn't allow us to see what's right in front of us— to be grateful for all the things we have that so many others don't.

I am grateful that in the last five years, I have been able to travel to Haiti, Africa, and India twenty-three times to serve and to learn. I was in Haiti seven times after the earthquake in 2010. Following the earthquake, Haiti was the poorest country in the world. I'd never seen more dire poverty in my life. And yet the children there were all laughing and playing— grateful to be chasing garbage around in a field.

I recently spent two three-week periods visiting an orphanage in India where every single one of the kids was mentally or physically handicapped ... or both. They had been left in garbage dumps, left for dead, and then they were brought to this orphanage called Happy Home to be fed, given healthcare, educated, and loved in the name of Jesus. And it is the happiest place I have ever been in the world. The orphanage is run by a twenty-seven-year-old Indian man named Roshan, his American wife, Rose, and his mother, Irene. They care for a hundred kids twenty-four hours a day, seven days a week, 365 days a year. They are always on, serving these kids.

In the first twenty minutes at Happy Home, you will be bawling your eyes out, overwhelmed by the feeling of love. You walk into a little room, and these forgotten, abandoned, "disabled" kids are singing at the top of their lungs, smiling. And when you walk in, they all gather around you, shake your hand, hug you, love you, and pray for you— all within the first twenty minutes of your arrival.

These children are the poorest of the poor. They are the ones whom everybody has forgotten. Yet they are so, so grateful. They have a warm place to sleep. They have food to eat. They have clothes to wear. They know the love of these caretakers. They know the love of God. These are kids who have nothing. They are five-, ten-, fifteen-, and twenty-year-olds whose families have left them, whose relatives are all dead, who were left in a garbage dump for dead. And they are the happiest people I have ever met—and I'm a pretty happy person myself!

There's a little girl with beautiful eyes and beautiful black hair, and she's smiling and singing at the top of her lungs songs of thanksgiving to God. That is gratitude. That is what changes the world. I am grateful for what these kids have taught me about what is really important in life.

When my clients are truly finding it impossible to come up with three things they are grateful for, I'll play a game with them. I tell them that we can trade things we are grateful for, and I tell them that I will go first. "I am grateful that it rained here today," I'll say, "because with the severe heat, we really needed it." I will start with something that simple, that small—because that is where gratitude starts.

Learning to be grateful requires rewiring your brain, your heart, and your soul. It's very simple. It's just changing the way that you think so that your first instinct is gratitude. For far too many people, the first instinct, the first reaction to any situation, is *What's in it for me? What can I get? What don't I have?* Instead of thinking that, start with, What am I grateful for? What have I been given that I don't deserve?

I was born in America. I could have been born in Haiti or Uganda or India, and I could be living in poverty. I could have been sold into slavery. I could be sick. I could be dead. Instead, I am here. Just that simple fact is something to be grateful for. I don't let myself get caught up in the negative image of our country that I see on the news, all the stories about how bad our country is. Instead, I focus on how grateful I am that my tutor was able to go to university in New York to learn to teach her son and to learn how to work with people with learning difficulties. I am grateful that she had the freedom to go and become educated and learn and create new ideas, because those opportunities don't exist everywhere. If she had been born in Iraq or Afghanistan or any number of places in the world, she would never have been allowed to go to school, and I would never have benefitted from her education.

Once you start focusing on gratitude, everything will start to change. Your mind is brilliant. As soon as you shift your focus, you will start to see things differently. You will start to be grateful for your own strengths and your own God-given abilities. If you are grateful, you will appreciate who you are, your own uniqueness, and your God-given ability. When you start to appreciate that, then you start to value it. You start to see that you can make a difference. You start to see that you can have an impact on a community, a school, a business, your family, your spouse, or your kids. When you can change yourself, you can change the world.

When you change the way you see yourself, you change the way you think about yourself. You start to believe that you have a contribution to make. You have a reason for being. God does not make junk. We are all valuable.

We all have a role. We all have a purpose. We all can make a difference.

I had a client recently who had no idea what his God-given ability might be. While speaking with him, he recounted a story about an occasion four or five years ago when he went to lunch with one of his managers. After the lunch, the manager said to him, "What you just did for me was amazing. I feel so encouraged. I am so motivated. Now I can do this project. Now I know that I'm going to be able to really get my team going."

Despite this amazing feedback from his manager, my client didn't capture what his manger was saying—that my client had a natural, God-given ability to motivate and inspire—so he didn't spend any time investing in those abilities. During our sessions, he finally realized that he could make this a focus of his life, and he could really start leading a life centered on his God-given ability. It was a huge breakthrough. His mindset started to change.

The entire process began with gratitude and tallying the simple things he was grateful for: having a roof over his head, having a car, having a job. But within a week to ten days, he had remembered and keyed into that experience with his manager, and had come to a new perspective on his life and on himself. He had found his way to change the world.

How far are we, really, from changing the world? In our own minds, it can seem impossible. We listen to all the people who say, "It is too difficult. Don't even try." But in truth, all you need is a slight adjustment toward grateful thinking.

You may look at the people in the world who have accomplished great things and think, *Well that's amazing, but I could never do that.* And you are right—it's not something you can do, because you are not that person. It's not your God-given ability. You don't have the God-given ability they have ... and they do not have the God-given ability, God-given passion, and God-given mission you have. You can't compare yourself to other people. You have to find your own unique, God-given ability. And then, instead of comparing yourself to other people, you can team up with them and achieve great things together.

Gratitude can change every part of your life. Think about the best relationship you have in your life—whether it's with your spouse, a parent, a sibling, your best friend, a teammate or a co-worker. Now imagine what would happen if, every time you saw that person, you started the conversation by exchanging the things about each other for which you are grateful today. And imagine that when your time together came to an end, you did it again, sharing what you are grateful for about each other right at that moment. Imagine what that relationship would feel like in six months, a year, or two years. You love that person now, but imagine how much fuller that love could be if you were to practice that gratitude every time you see him or her. I challenge you to stop, put this book down, and do what I just said in this paragraph.

Gratitude is powerful not just when it is felt, but when it is expressed. When you convey gratitude, you change not just yourself, but everything around you. Think about a stressful work situation, one in which a relationship is strained and both parties are on edge. Imagine if the people having the conflict took the time to write down three things they were grateful for and appreciate about the other person, and give it to that person. It would fix so many problems, and it would allow people to work toward common solutions rather than toward further conflicts.

We have a holiday in the United States called Thanksgiving. The sad truth is that many people spend this holiday fighting with their relatives. Now imagine what would happen if the first thing you did when you sat down at the table for Thanksgiving dinner was give thanks. It's a simple exercise: before you eat, turn to the person on your right and say all the things you are grateful for about them. Then they turn to the person on their right and do the same. Then, once you've gone around the table, flip and go the other way. I guarantee you the conversation over Thanksgiving dinner and for the rest of the evening will be infinitely more loving and enjoyable for everyone. Out of gratitude comes appreciation, and what we appreciate becomes valued, and what we value we treat with love and respect.

If you are grateful for people and the help they give you, they will want to continue helping you. I am always amazed by all the people who have helped me in my life. For years, I couldn't figure out why people were willing to help me, why they were willing to sacrifice their time to come to my assistance. And then I realized that part of it was because I was always grateful. I always sent a thank-you card—a message telling them how much I appreciated them. I tell others how grateful I am to have them in my life, and it has made a world of difference.

My father was severely dyslexic. Reading or writing anything was incredibly difficult for him. Right before he died, he sent me a note. It probably took him ten days to write, and he had probably written it over a thousand times. It was very simple. It read, "Thank you for all your love and support. Love, Dad." It is one of my most cherished possessions.

I have never felt more appreciated and grateful in my life. It was just a simple note, but it changed me.

That is how you change the world: one person at a time, simply by being grateful. And it all starts with merely writing down three things you are grateful for right now. Will you choose a life of gratitude today?

CHAPTER THREE

Why I'm Financially Free

I grew up visiting my father's brothers in the prisons of California. Some of them were there for life. Some of them died there. All of them — as well as my father and grandfather — were dyslexic. The only difference between my father and them, the only reason my father was with me while my uncles were in prison, is that my father *made a choice* to follow a different path.

Around the globe, the percentage of prison inmates who suffer from learning disabilities is incredibly high. Close to 60 percent of prison inmates have some kind of learning disability— dyslexia, ADD, ADHD, Asperger's syndrome, etc.

For people with learning difficulties, the path to prison starts in kindergarten. When I was growing up, the educational system in this country did not have any protocols for handling somebody like me, somebody with a learning disability. There was no place for me. I was lucky enough to have someone in my life who could help me—my remarkable tutor.
But back then, atypical children who were dependent on the educational system and didn't benefit from the intervention of a teacher, parent, or someone else were completely left out. They experienced humiliation and bullying, and were pushed further and further away from the educational

system. And in the United States, the educational system leads children into careers and into the rest of their lives.

People who have gone through this— who have gone through so much failure and so much rejection in the standard system—feel they have no choice but to look for options outside of the system. They may start hanging out with other people who don't follow that system. And unfortunately for many people, that path leads to a life of bad choices.

How do you become a bank robber? Not by saying, out of the blue, "Hey, I'm going to rob a bank." It happens over many years, and the process is driven by the many choices you make and by the people around you. Pretty soon, some of the people you associate with are saying, "Well, would you drive the car?" And you think, "It's okay, I'm just driving the car. I'm not really a part of it." But the path continues, and eventually you find yourself in prison.

The choices you make accumulate and become your life's path. Without support, encouragement, and guidance toward a positive path— without people saying, "We believe in you"— it can be very easy to stray onto a path that leads to the streets or to prison. And once you start down that path, it can be extremely hard to get off it. Once you've gone to prison, chances are you will go back. Over half of all people who serve time in prison end up back in prison.

It's almost impossible to make positive choices when everyone around you, all day long, every day of the year, has the mentality that crime is the only path available. It can be easy to feel like there is no other answer when you've failed in school, when you're told that you are a loser, that you are dumb.

We need to look at children from when they are in kindergarten all the way through high school, and ask ourselves: is it worth investing in them? Is it worth believing in them, encouraging them, giving them the tools and resources they need to find their own genius and their own God-given abilities, so that they can find their own positive paths? Or are we just going to throw them to the curb?

Because someone intervened on my behalf and because I was encouraged and supported by the people around me, I didn't spend all my time, energy, and focus on what I couldn't do or on the areas where I was failing. Instead, I was able to use my God-given ability to build the skills that would carry me in the real world, where people care about results. I realized that I could generate results in a unique way because I could make people believe in themselves, and I had a knack for surrounding myself with super-smart people. Thanks to these abilities, we were able to build a company and I was able to become financially free, and not end up in prison.

If you find yourself on the path to prison—or even if your path has already led you there—you can start changing your mindset and making different choices. It's as simple as what I did when I woke up this morning: I made a choice to do and to think and to live and to be a person who is going to make a great impact on the world today.

Every morning, I wake up and think, "What are the things I can do today that will have the greatest impact?" One of my gifts—my God-given abilities—is encouragement, so one of the first things I think in the morning is, "How can I encourage the world today?"

Finding a better path is all about thinking. Our mind does not control us; we control our mind. Many people don't realize that they are actually in control of the supercomputer in their head. They let their mind take them wherever it wants to go rather than consciously thinking and making choices. And for most people, myself included, if we don't consciously choose to do positive things— to be all that we are supposed to be— our mind will lead us to making bad choices instead. Our mind will say, "I'm not going to get up and go to work today. I don't feel like it. I'm going to call in sick." Or, "I'm not going to do my homework. I'm going to go hang out on the corner with those guys who are not good characters."

Changing your life's path can seem like a huge, unattainable goal, but it starts with a very simple task, a tool that I give to my clients to help them change their choices and the way they think. The task is easy. First, every morning, say to yourself,

"What are the three achievements I'm going to go after today?" Not a million achievements; just three things that are going to change your own world in the biggest way you can with your God-given ability. Then, at the end of the day, before you go to sleep, take inventory of the day's experiences you are grateful for, the people you are grateful for, and what you were able to contribute to the world that day.

The thing that causes many people to get stuck—and that has gotten me stuck many times—is that when making these choices today, it can be hard to see how your life is going to change. It's very easy to feel like nothing will make a difference, that your life is never going to change. But it can. I know, because it happened to me.

I experienced ten years of failure between the ages of twenty and thirty. I failed at everything I tried to do. But I made the choice with every one of my failures to learn more about how to be a successful entrepreneur, a better husband, and a better father. I kept educating myself, learning, and asking questions.

For ten years, I was going backward so fast it scared everybody except my wife and me. When I was thirty-two, I had three small children, and my daughter had a major medical problem. We didn't have insurance because we couldn't afford it, and despite the fact that both my wife and I worked, we were living on little to nothing. We consulted a bankruptcy attorney, and when we laid everything out for him, he looked at us and said, "I have never seen anybody so upside-down financially in my life. You owe one hundred thousand dollars and you're only making nine hundred dollars a month. You need to stop and quit. You need to declare bankruptcy. I'm not even going to charge you a fee because I feel so bad about what has happened to you."

Despite the attorney's shock, my wife and I decided not to file for bankruptcy. Neither one of us believed that it was the right thing to do. For the next four or five years, we continued making choices that we felt would lead us to a brighter future, without any results to show for it. But we knew we had to become the people we were meant to be and do the things we had always dreamed about. I knew, because of my life experiences up to that point, that I had a God-given ability in me. And my wife believed in me too— often even more than I believed in myself. *I realized that God is not against us, but for us in this life.*

Between the two of us, we became an invincible team. We were unbeatable, even though by the world's standards, we were a total wreck. Our parents looked at us and said, "This is getting worse. We feel so bad." I worked eighty hours a week—as a janitor and cleaning up at construction sites. My wife worked as a secretary. We had three little kids and we lived in a rented house; it seemed like our cars broke down every week. Everything that could go wrong went wrong.

And yet, between the two of us, and with *God's constant encouragement*, we knew that something amazing was going to happen. For ten years, we lived on this belief that God had prepared us for an amazing life. Not ten minutes, not ten hours, not ten days, not ten months. Ten years. But we believed.

Most important, my wife believed in me. She was the real hero. I would never have survived without her telling me, over and over again, how much she believed in me. She told me that there was something great in me, and that there was a great future in store for us if we just stuck with it and stayed in the game. Every morning when I woke up, she told me she believed in me. And every night when I went to sleep, she told me she believed in me. She wrote me notes and called me during the day to say, "It's going to happen. It's right around the corner. Today, let's try again. Let's try something else. Let's keep trying." In the thirty-six years we have been together, she has never, either verbally or non-verbally, questioned or doubted me. It is a true miracle that I have her in my life, and that I have had her in my life for so long.

When you have somebody on your side—be it a spouse, parent, child, friend, or co-worker—who constantly tells you that they believe in you, you start to believe. Even when everything around you is a disaster, even when everyone around you tells you to stop, if you have someone who

believes in you then you can start to
see glimpses of brilliance. You start
to have flashes of your God-given
ability, your God-given purpose, and
your God-given mission. It starts
to come to the surface in different
situations. You start to feel it
moving through you.

You have to be very careful who
you listen to and what you believe,
because what you believe will come
true. During my freshman year of
high school, I was told that the only
occupation in the world that I was
qualified for was to be a janitor. I
took the test, and it came back with
only one answer. My teacher told me
he'd never seen anything like it, but it
was clear that the only thing I could
ever hope to be was a janitor.

And for seven years, when I was
in my twenties and thirties, that is
exactly what I was. For a time, I
believed that it was the only thing I

could do. And because I believed it, it became true. During these years of hardship, I worked all day cleaning up at construction sites. Then at night, I cleaned office buildings until four in the morning. I did this for five or six years. I barely slept, and it started to show. Sometimes when driving home at four o'clock in the morning, I would start to fall asleep at the wheel. Once I was woken up by a policeman who told me I had been going the wrong way down the freeway on the median. I didn't realize it because I'd fallen asleep. My body just couldn't function on the schedule I kept.

Through all of this, and especially after that harrowing experience, I thought and prayed: "Please God, there must be something else that I can do that would better provide for my family, something I could do in the long term." I knew, even at twenty-seven and twenty-eight years old, that I would not physically be able to

do this for the rest of my life. I didn't
know how much longer I could continue
to keep those hours. I was only in my
twenties, but I felt like I was fifty
years old.

The nature of the jobs I worked meant
I spent almost all of my time alone.
Sixteen, eighteen, twenty hours a
day by myself. And that whole time,
I talked to God, praying for God to
show me a better way, some other
way to live.

Then, over the course of one year, I
had three separate people come to me
and say, "I think you would be a really
great insurance guy."

This was the last thing I would ever
have thought of for myself. It had
never even crossed my mind. When
the first person said that to me, I
responded, "I don't think that's me. I
don't know where you got that idea,
but that's crazy." But soon afterward,

another person came to me and said the same thing.

I went home to my wife and told her, "I've got all these people talking to me about insurance. I'm a janitor. It's crazy. Why would they think that?"

Then a third person, somebody I really respected, came to me and said, "I think you should look into getting into insurance."

When that happened, I said, "Well, I may be slow, but God keeps sending people to me. It sounds crazy, but I guess I'd better at least look into this."

I investigated what it would take to get into insurance. I immediately found out that to get a license, you have to take a class and an exam. Moreover, the class and exam were quite expensive. "There's no way I could ever do this," I said to my wife. "You have to read all this material, and it's all this technical stuff. It's not even English. The industry has its own language. I can't even read English, so how am I supposed to read a whole other language?"

My wife was understanding. "Let's think about it," she said; "Let's pray about it." Some time passed. Then my wife said to me, "You know, I think you should do it."

I still wasn't convinced. I came up with another excuse. "The class is a hundred and fifty dollars," I told her. "And then you have to pay a fee to the state to take an exam. It's two hundred dollars, all told. We don't have two hundred dollars." My wife was not dissuaded. Somehow, over the next month or so, we managed to come up with two hundred dollars.

So I took the class. It was lecture-based, with a whole stack of notes and books. I was sweating. I felt like I was back in school. What am I doing here? I thought. This is insane. But it was only a week long, so I stuck with it.

Finally, the week ended, and it was time for the exam. I went to the testing center, only to discover that the test was conducted on a computer. At that point in my life, I had never even seen a computer, let alone used one. I thought that was the end. But I steeled myself, went up to the lady at the testing center and said, "Ma'am, I do not know how to use these computers."

Thankfully, the lady was incredibly nice. "Don't worry," she said. "Nobody else is here. I'll show you how it works. It's very simple. All you have to do is click two buttons." She showed me how the program worked,

and then said, "You have two and a half hours to take the test."
Great, I thought, *That's a lot of time. I should be able to finish ... I hope ...*

I sat down at the computer and started the test, and something very strange happened: I was overcome with a weird sensation, and I finished the test in fifty-five minutes. All of a sudden, there was the screen in front of me asking me to click a button to confirm that I was finished.

I have failed more tests than most people will ever take in their lives, so I had a bad feeling. When I came out of the testing room, my fears were confirmed. "Do you have to go to the bathroom?" the lady asked. "Or did you have a question?"

"No," I said, "I'm done."

"You can't be done," the lady replied. "It takes two and a half hours."

"No, ma'am" I said, my heart sinking, "I'm done."

"Oh my gosh," she said sympathetically. "That's not good."

I wasn't surprised. I had gotten that feeling as soon as I finished. "Well, okay," the lady said. "I can't refund you the money, you know."

"I know," I said. It was a total disaster, exactly as I had expected.

Since the test was on a computer, my score was available immediately. "Let me pull up your results," the lady said. As she did, I braced myself for the hard truth. The lady looked down at her computer screen, and then looked at me with a puzzled expression on her face. It looked like the expression I'd seen a thousand times before on the face of every teacher I'd ever had. "You failed," I knew she was going to say. "You have to retake the test. You have to do the class over. You flunked."

I sighed and started heading to the door. And then the lady spoke. "You have a seventy-one," she said.

I stopped. "What does that mean?"

"You only need to have a seventy to pass," the lady said. "You have a seventy-one. You passed. You are now a licensed agent."

I could not believe it. I thought I must have misheard. "Well, I'm going to go," I said.

"No, no," she said. "You have to go down to the state house and get your certificate and your license. You passed the test."

"Are you sure?" I asked. "I don't mean to be rude, but are you sure the computer is right, or that you're reading it right?"

"The computer is exact. Here, you can see which questions you got right. You got seventy-one percent right. You're done. You met the standard."

So there it was: I could actually get a license. Now, for a lot of people, that might not seem like much. But to me, it was a sign. Maybe there was something there. Maybe there was something more I could be doing.

After getting my license, I found a company in the newspaper and started work as a sales representative. I was trained, and then I started meeting with potential customers. I found that I was getting a lot of negative feedback about the products. Of course I thought that it was me, that I was just a bad salesman.

Then I started talking to another agent at the company who was having a similar experience. "I've done some research," he said, "and there are other products that are better than what we are offering. It's so terrible that I'm thinking of leaving the company." We wanted to continue the conversation, so we made plans to get lunch.

Unfortunately, our manager overheard us making our lunch plans. "Can I come with you?" he asked. That wasn't great for us since we wanted to talk about leaving, but we didn't want to refuse our manager. We agreed that he could come along.

At lunch, our manager talked about the company's products. It turned out that he had done some research himself, and he'd found a better product from the East Coast—and he wanted to sell it. As our manager talked, the other agent and I got excited. And by the end of the lunch, there at the table, we made a partnership with a hundred dollars. We started our own business.

We all had our own skills and abilities that we brought to the business, and mine was the ability to recruit, motivate, change, inspire, and teach the people we brought on board. We started with just the three of us at a table, and we grew to an agency that sold in forty-two states and, within our niche, was one of the top-producing agencies in the entire country. Within six or seven years, I went from absolute poverty to the upper one tenth of one percent of the country. And most important, I had started to truly find myself.

All of this happened because I took that leap of faith. I faced my ultimate fear—going back to school—and enrolled in that class. I took that exam—and I succeeded. It gave me so much confidence, enthusiasm, and passion. I found that I loved the insurance business because it was all about people. I loved our customers, all of whom were entrepreneurs and business owners. I knew how to help them, and I was good at it. All I had to do was find the right vehicle. I never stopped trying to learn, trying to understand, trying to say, "Okay, what is it that I can do? What contribution can I make?"

None of this would have happened without people believing in me. My wife, my parents, my friends, and my partners always believed that there was something out there for me, and that made me believe in myself.

Now, you may be reading this and feeling like you don't have that person in your life who will believe in you no matter what, and who will keep telling you to believe. I am here to say that I am that person. I believe in you. I'm here, and I believe in you.

No matter where you are, wherever you've come from, whatever problems you are dealing with—I believe in you, probably more than you believe in yourself. I stand with you. I love you. And I believe that you have something amazing in you and that you will do amazing things. That is my purpose, my legacy, and my mission: to believe in you. That is my God-given ability: to help you find yours.

When I woke up this morning, I said, "God, please send me more people, people whom I can encourage." It's why I visit prisons—I want to understand the inmates who have learning disabilities. I know what happened in their childhood, how they strayed onto the path that led them to prison. I recently visited a prison in Uganda and spoke with 354 men and women. I was the only person who had come in there this year and told them, "I love you. I believe in you. I believe that God has a plan for you. I believe there is something you can be doing to change the world."

I know that within every prisoner is a gift, a contribution. There is a role for them in society, and if given the chance to fulfill that role, they could be amazingly productive. But unfortunately, in our society we too often look at those people and think because they don't fit in the one-size-fits-all system, we have to throw them out like garbage.

That's why I go to prisons, schools, universities, hospitals, and clinics. I have traveled to Haiti, India, and Africa to meet with people. I want those people to know that somebody understands and cares. I believe that every single one of them can come out of their situation and do something amazing.

Everybody in the world, no matter the challenges they face and no matter how hopeless things seem, has something amazing to offer to the world. I know this because it's my story. I get it. I was the kid in the corner who was forgotten. I was the teenager who was told the only thing he could ever hope to be was a janitor. I was a married father of three who was told that I was bankrupt beyond belief. But I believed, and I had people who believed in me.

I believe. I believe that all the world's people have something great within them, something to contribute, and something they can live out every day. No matter how alone you feel, you are not alone. There are people in the world who believe in you. There are people in the world who have your back. And I'm one of them. Even though I don't know you personally, I love you, and I believe in you.

CHAPTER FOUR

Everything I Need to Know About Business I Learned in Sixth Grade

When I was in sixth grade, around the year 1970, I had a revolutionary teacher named Mr. Bakala. On the first day of class, the first thing he said to us was, "I want you to remove all the desks from the classroom." I knew then and there I was in for something brand new. "We're going to do something totally different," said Mr. Bakala. It was his very first year teaching, and he was going to shake things up.

So we cleared all the furniture out of the classroom, and we sat down on rugs. I didn't know what to think. I had been having such a miserable time in school as it was, and now here was this crazy teacher changing everything up on me.

Mr. Bakala explained: "I know that people learn in a lot of different ways, by a lot of different methods. So this year, we're going to try learning in different kinds of ways." He said that one of the things we were going to do was turn the classroom into a business. Everybody started out with a little bit of money—the equivalent of about fifty dollars—and then we were each required to provide a service for the class. This could be renting the balls for recess, making copies, or checking out books. We would all learn what it was like to be a businessperson.

This was a completely cutting-edge way of teaching in that era, especially in a small, conservative town of only ten to twelve thousand people. It took a lot of guts to depart from the traditional educational methods to which we were accustomed.

Looking back, it's pretty amazing, and I can truly appreciate what a remarkable teacher Mr. Bakala was. He made learning a game, and he related it to the real world, so it was more than just book learning. He wanted to show us how things really worked.

At first, I was skeptical. The first week, I went home and told my parents, "Brace yourselves. It's going to start all over again." I was really upset because just when I was starting to get some traction with the basic reading and writing stuff, this guy was throwing it all out the window. I was convinced that it was going to be worse than ever, and that I would fail even harder than I had before.

It didn't take long for me to figure out that I had a good mind for business in a way that most of the other kids didn't. Somehow, I was getting it, even as the straight-A kids couldn't figure out how it worked. I realized that one of my God-given abilities, one of the things I really had a mind for, was business— how it works, how to leverage ideas, how to invest and get a return, and then take that return and invest in something else. I understood money, and I understood that money is about acceleration— the faster you can move it from place to place, the faster you can make more.

As the year went on, I underwent a metamorphosis because of what I was learning in Mr. Bakala's classroom.

It was amazing. In all my years in school, I had been told that learning was defined as getting good grades and doing well on my math tests and English papers. Now here was this teacher telling me that what we were doing, this business thing that I inherently understood, was actually what the real world was like. "This is how people make a living," he told us.

It sounds so simple, but for me it was a revelation. I was beyond excited. For the first time in my life, I saw that there was actually somewhere for me to go after school. If I could just get through school, I might actually have a chance to be successful in life. For the first time in seven years, I actually wanted to go to school in the morning.

My whole attitude changed, and I started to find myself. My confidence and self-esteem began to blossom. I tried out new things, and I discovered

that I was very good at sports. So
I started playing team sports at my
school, and even earned a Sportsman
of the Year award that year. I had
discovered that I really did have
abilities and strengths. For the
previous seven years, I had spent most
of my time doing the things that were
most difficult for me. Now, I was in
an environment where I was working
on things I was good at, and it was
incredibly empowering. I wanted to
learn more. I wanted to do more. I
wanted to own this and that business.
I wanted to invest in the little stock
market we ran in our classroom. I had
my hand in everything, from bringing
out the sports equipment for recess
to making copies to selling popcorn
from our little popcorn machine during
recess.

By the end of the year, I was a
hundred times richer than anybody
else in the class, and I basically had
a monopoly on our classroom's little

economy. I still couldn't read or write to save my life, but I understood the concept of business and was able to execute it successfully. And what's more, I could explain it and teach it to other people. I could actually help other people. I had never experienced that in my life.

When I left sixth grade, I began to focus on the fact that I could someday be a successful businessperson. I finally knew that there was something I could be successful at, something I had been given the ability to do. While I still took my algebra and English classes, I was no longer focused on the failures I faced in those classes. I knew that was not my future.

Instead, I started opening up little businesses outside of school. I went door to door selling walnuts. I ran carnivals in the summer. I found ways to make money—and I was good at it.

After sixth grade, I always had money. When I was in junior high, I used to run around with a hundred dollar bill in my wallet, which back then was no small amount. I was able to create businesses and make a profit because that's just the way I was wired.

It was uncanny how easily that kind of thinking came to me. I even started to get really good at Monopoly; in fact, I went undefeated for about ten years! To me, it was the easiest game in the world. I took on all challengers and I beat them all. I could even beat adults. I challenged people to put down five dollars on a game, and I always won.

I learned to put my energy into things at which I could be successful. That was a choice, and it was a choice of gratitude. I started saying to myself, I'm good at this. I'm grateful for it. I made a conscious choice to appreciate and

value being good at something, and
I learned to invest in my God-given
ability. And the things I wasn't good
at, I chose to ignore, because where
did they lead? To the same place
where most dyslexics are at my age:
they are depressed and discouraged;
they hate their jobs, and they
struggle in their relationships with
their families— all because they are
focusing on what they can't do
instead of on what they can.

Dyslexia doesn't go away. I'm fifty-
five years old and I still live with it
every day. I suffer disorientation all
the time. Just the other day I was
trying to put a whole bunch of stuff
together with my team— twenty-one
people, all in different groups, working
on different things for me— and I was
just not in my element. By the end of
the day, I was completely exhausted
and disoriented because I had been
operating all day outside the scope of
my God-given abilities.

I don't live in a fantasy world. I don't pretend there aren't challenges every single day. But I don't let disorientation define who I am or ruin my life. I am a work in progress. I constantly have to work to remind myself of why I am here. What is my role? What are my abilities? What is my purpose, my mission? What are these God-given things that I can bring to the world? And what choices am I going to make today to follow that path?

So many people are told that there is only one path to follow, only one path to success. I say that there are seven billion paths. And the only path you have to follow is your own. That is the only way to get to what I call "the Kingdom of Joy," a place of happiness, peace, and contentment. You can get to the Kingdom of Joy by being you, because you are amazing. You are a gift to the world. You have a purpose. And that is why it is so important for you to be yourself, and not try to be anybody else.

Hope is important for all of us. Whatever our situations may be, if we don't have hope, we'll shrivel up and die. Without hope, we may find ourselves on the path to prison. I don't know if Mr. Bakala has any idea just how much hope he instilled in me. That man was a true hero in my life.

I have three paperweights on my desk that were presents from my wife. One says "kindness," one says "charity," and one says "hope." For me, the greatest of the three is hope. There is no greater thing you can do for somebody than to give them hope, to believe in them, to encourage, support, and love them. My life experience has shown me that there is no greater gift in the world. And when I look at those three paperweights, I am reminded of all the people in my life who have provided me with hope, and I realize how fortunate I am.

I was very lucky to have had a teacher like Mr. Bakala who could help me find my way. But even if you don't have a revolutionary sixth-grade teacher, you can still find your own path. What it comes down to is a conversation you need to have with God.

I believe in miracles, and I don't believe in chance or coincidence. I believe there is a purpose for all of us. I think every person can have that conversation with God and say, "You put me here, so there must be a reason for it. Show me a way. Open the door. Reveal a path." And God will. He sent me those three people telling me to go into insurance, completely out of left field. You just have to open your mind up to the fact that there is another path out there for you. Even if you don't know what it is, it's out there.

CHAPTER FIVE

The Real Reasons Why You Are Unhappy with Your Life

Every Monday morning, 82 percent of the people in the world wake up and groan, "I have to do this again?" I hear this all the time. I hear it from business owners, from entrepreneurs, from students. All they want is to make it through to the weekend. They drag themselves to work, week after week, year after year, and they hate every day of it.

I can tell you the number one reason people are unhappy with their lives: it is because they are not finding any meaning in what they are doing. They're not finding any enjoyment. They're not finding any passion. They're not really doing what they were made to do, and they are not really using their true talents and abilities.

We spend up to 70 percent of our lives working. And the majority of people work doing something they are not passionate about, something they don't have the innate ability to do. When you are not fulfilled in your work life—when you are fundamentally unhappy with 70 or 80 percent of what you do every week, every year, year after year—the person who is closest to you is going to experience that negativity every single day, day after day, year after year. And the result is not going to be good. It is no wonder divorce rates are so high.

One recent morning I was meeting with a sales rep. He's been a sales rep for twenty years, and he told me, "I can't do this anymore." And I agreed with him. His health was starting to fail. His marriage was becoming more and more strained. He felt like he didn't know his two kids. This didn't happen in a day. It happened over twenty years of him not living to be who he was, not living in his passion, in his purpose, in his God-given ability.

I understand what it's like to be this unhappy. I've been on the other side. I've been in that situation where I was not in my element. I trudged through fifteen years of school when it just didn't work for me, when it was not the way I functioned, and I was miserable. When I was only eight years old, I wanted to take my own life. But really, all I was saying was, "Help me. Help me figure it out."

And I know that I could easily be in the same position today. I live a mile away from one of the largest Intel manufacturing and engineering locations in the world. At this facility, twenty-five thousand engineers work to make smaller and smaller microchips. My whole neighborhood is filled with brilliant people who are working at something they're really good at. But if I were working at that Intel facility, I would not be using my God-given ability. I would not be using my passion. And I can guarantee you that I would be unhappy in my work.

If you are part of that 82 percent, I have good news for you: It doesn't have to be that way. Your work can feed your soul. You can find work or business that is meaningful to you. You can have peace, happiness, and contentment in your work, and that goodness will overflow into every other part of your life.

This country was established on the premise that people are able to be who they are and believe what they want to believe. The founding generations of this country worked hard and sacrificed to follow their dreams. In 1904 my grandmother walked with a wagon train from St. Louis, Missouri, all the way to Oregon to make a new life. It was not an easy journey; half the people who made the trip with her died along the way. But they were intent on following their dreams.

People have immigrated to this country for centuries in an effort to pursue their own passions and dreams. It's what this country is built on. Before she died, my grandmother talked to me about how much joy and purpose there was in her life, despite all the hardships. She truly lived her life, and truly followed her dreams. I believe that our society today has strayed from that sense of joy and purpose. We've become enamored with the kind of "success" we see on TV, with movie stars and pop stars and sports stars. Our culture holds up so many icons, so many idols, and we aspire to be like these people. We strive to be like them, instead of striving to be ourselves. Whether it's Sir Richard Branson or President Obama or Oprah Winfrey, we are always striving to be like somebody else. Trying to be like somebody else is incredibly frustrating, and incredibly disappointing. Why? Because you are not somebody else. You are yourself. You need to strive to be your best self. When you try to be something or somebody you are not, you will always fall short. The vast majority of us are not going to be movie stars or pop stars or sports stars. But we can be stars in our own lives, with our own God-given abilities.

Instead of striving to be like someone else, you need to sit down and say, "What are the things that give me life? What are the experiences that bring me joy? What just makes me super stoked? What doesn't feel like work when I do it, even though it is work? And why don't I arrange my life so that I'm spending 50, 60, or 70 percent of my time doing that thing and being who I was meant to be?"

I saw a young gentleman recently who had been working in the high-tech industry for a long time, and had just been laid off. At first, he saw this as a terrible thing. Then after a few conversations, he said to me, "You know, I've got to be honest with you. I always really wanted to work in the animation field, but I've never done it. But that's what I want to pursue. I've spent ten years doing something I'm not really passionate about, and it's made me a person that I'm not really pleased with. I'm not heading in the right direction."

This client was finally able to be honest and say that what he had been doing was not the right fit. He was able to say, "This is what I'm actually passionate about." He had spent ten years going to work every day and then coming home and building games, because that was his passion. But he had never pursued his passion, never made his passion his priority. Now, because he was being honest with himself, he could start to make changes, start to live in his God-given ability.

That is the first step: being honest with yourself. It is incredibly simple, but it is also incredibly difficult. In fact, it is probably the hardest step of all. If you've worked somewhere for twenty years, if you've worked your way up, if you are a business owner, if you are "successful" in your job, it can be hard to admit that what you have been working for is not what brings meaning to your life. Admitting that honestly is a huge step to take.

But once you take that step, once you are honest with yourself, you can start to do an inventory, a self-evaluation. That is when you have to say, "I'm here for a reason. What is that reason? What do I have that I can give to the world? How can I create value out of my God-given ability?"

It's a scary thing to look in a mirror and ask, "What is it I was made for? What is it that I'm passionate about? What are my gifts and abilities, and how do I live them out—for the next ten years, twenty years, thirty or forty years?" Or if you are in college, to say, "How do I make sure that my work life for the next forty, fifty, sixty years is going to be fulfilling?

That it will have meaning? That it will have purpose? How is this part of my legacy?"

Your work is going to be a huge, huge part of your life. That pressure to find the right thing for yourself is incredibly intimidating, especially because unlike my young client and his passion for animation, you may not know exactly what industry you want to be in, or even exactly what you are passionate about. You may not be able to see how something you enjoy or are good at could translate into an actual job or business, into something you could actually do with your life. The truth is, your passion and ability may be something that isn't necessarily tied to any specific field. You may harness your God-given ability to create a new industry, product, or service.

I love the clients who come to me and say, "I have no idea what that thing is. I have no idea what my mission is, my purpose, my ability." Because that is not an easy thing to say. It takes real courage. But it is the first step.

It is exactly that uncertainty that I dealt with when I started to find my God-given ability. My God-given ability is to encourage people, to give them hope, to help them create a vision of a better life. Encouraging people? What job is that? What industry is that? It's not engineering, or music, or teaching, or animation. What could a life lived with the God-given ability to encourage people possibly look like?

It took some work to figure it out. It took some research. But most of all, it took me asking those questions. And I discovered that I could create a business out of encouraging people—I could become a coach. Now my job is to help you find your God-given ability and find how to live in it.

My job is to encourage you, to hold you accountable, to ask the tough questions. My job is to build your confidence in yourself, and to make you use your creative abilities in ways you hadn't thought about.

Don't just think about what job you want or what job you might be good at. Think about what you are good at that makes you happy. If you just try to think about what job you want, you will get stuck very quickly, and you may never find what truly makes you live out your mission.

And don't worry— you don't have to figure it out all by yourself. Once you are honest, you become vulnerable, and when you are vulnerable, you can ask people in your life— people who know you— what they see in you. You can ask, "What do you see in me that I'm not seeing?"

"You know," they might say, "I noticed that when we were working on this project, you really showed leadership in this way." Or, "You seem to have an innate ability to organize these types of projects in the community." Or, "I can always count on you because you always get all the details right." Those kinds of insights can help you find your way to your God-given ability.

Once you figure out what your God-given ability is, you can start to develop a plan. You can develop a God-given ability statement. And then you can say, "Okay, what jobs or work or business or companies or industries are out there that this ability would be of value to? Where could I be working where 50 percent of my work would use my God-given ability?"

When you make this shift, it can certainly be a struggle. You've been in another world for a year, for ten years, for twenty years. You have commitments and expenses. There will be many things to figure out as you make the transition. That can be incredibly scary, and it's okay to be afraid. Use that fear to give yourself energy for the transition. These changes take work and time. You may have to live differently in order to live out your God-given purpose, your God-given mission. You may have to sacrifice some things. But when you find something that you are really gifted at and passionate about that gives you great satisfaction, you have to be willing to make those sacrifices.

Many people are not willing to take this step. They are stuck in mediocrity and malaise, but they are not motivated enough to believe that there can be a better way of living, that there can be more meaning in their lives. They never change their input. They never think about things in a different way.

People settle all the time. But there is so much more that you could do. We settle for mediocrity because we want to keep this house or this car; to live in this neighborhood or go on this vacation. You may feel you've made choices that have put you into a position in life where you feel you can't change. Maybe you decided to have five kids instead of one. Maybe you've bought a house and it has you strapped. Whatever it is, it's making you feel like you can't make a change. It's making you feel like you can't go to night school and learn how to be an architect, if that is your God-given ability. But the truth is, you can. You always can.

If you are going to change your life, if you are going to find meaning and purpose and passion and joy and

happiness in relation to your work—
which will affect your family life,
your community life, and all your
relationships—then you have to be
willing to take that step. There are
going to be periods of fear, periods
of pain, periods of discomfort. There
are going to periods of transition
and uncertainty. But if you are
willing to get through those periods,
you will be able to get to a place
where you are not waking up on
Monday morning dreading the week.
You will get to a place where you
are actually excited about things
that are going to happen in your
work. You are going to feel like
you are making a difference in the
world you live in. You are going
to grow into your new role, to see
new opportunities, and to keep
getting excited about your life. Your
confidence, courage, and character
will grow strong and healthy.

The truth is, the result is far more
than just money. It will affect how

you feel about yourself, how you feel about what is happening in your life, and how you feel about the world. It won't just feed your bank account; it will feed your soul.

All these steps are scary, and it's okay to be scared. But you can't let that fear stop you. The mind is controlled by only two things, and you can only think of one of those things at a time: fear or faith. That's it. And we as a society are stuck in a culture of fear. We all have so much fear. I believe we all also have an inkling of the greatness within us, but we are afraid of it.

We say, "Who am I to think that I could be great? Who am I to think that I could change the world?" I know this feeling well. I'm a nobody from a small town. I'm not educated. I can barely read. Where do I get off telling you that you have greatness in you, that you can change the world? Where does that come from?

It comes from inside me. I not only believe it; I've actually lived it out. I've actually experienced it. I was able to come from absolutely nothing, and I found that thing that is my God-given ability, my God-given passion, and my God-given mission.

That is the side of faith. The faith side says, "Yes, there is something you can do. You are not garbage. You are not junk. You can make a huge difference in the world."

It all starts with being honest about where you are and who you are. Be honest about the choices you've made. Then have the guts to be vulnerable, the guts to say, "I'm going to do something today to start changing, so that a year from now, five years from now, ten years from now, I can live out this purpose, this mission, this ability that I have. I can live this life of gratitude, this life of joy, this life of waking up and feeling that there is meaning to my day. Instead of being unhappy, I can be excited. Instead of my days draining me, they can fill me up, and I can pour myself into life." Instead of waking up unhappy with your life, you can wake up overjoyed.

CHAPTER SIX

Who's Really Disabled—
Valedictorians and Prom Queens,
or People Like You and Me?

All our lives, we are shown examples of success. We are shown valedictorians and prom queens, movie stars and celebrities. For those of us who have a so-called "disability," it can be incredibly disheartening. We can start to feel like there is no way for us ever to be truly successful.

I have a different way of looking at things. In my view, we are not the ones who are disabled; in fact, those very models of "success" are the ones who should be considered disabled!

Before you dismiss me as completely crazy, let me explain what I mean.

I believe failure at a young age—as young as in your school years—is actually the best teacher and best preparer for your adult years. As a child, I became an expert in failing fast. I would take a test, and the teacher would give me an F. I would take it again and get an F. I would take it again and maybe get a D. Eventually, the teacher would get tired and just let me move on. The practice of persistence became a quality which eventually won out.

The result of this constant failure was that I learned to put failure behind me very quickly. I would take what I could away from the experience, learn everything that would help me, and I would put it behind me. When I was

just a kid— six, eight, ten, fourteen
years old— I learned to deal with
setbacks and failures. I was learning
at a level that most people don't
learn at until they are in their fifties.
I was earning my Masters and PhD in
failure, and those lessons helped me
to succeed in my adult life.
It wasn't until my high school years
that I realized that all this failure
might actually be a blessing. That's
when I started to realize that it
might actually be pretty tough for
all those straight-A kids when they
got out of the school system and
entered the real world. For the prom
queens and the valedictorians, the
academic culture is built to support
the way they operate. As a result,
they experience only one thing in their
childhood and early lives: success. The
problem is, when you get out in the
real world, most of those things don't
transfer. It's not the same system.
It's not about grades; it's about
results.

The people who achieved so much
success in the academic system were
taught to believe that they would
always be successful, no matter what.
They learned through their experiences
that they would always win in life.
The fact is, that is just not true.
They do have setbacks and failures,
and they don't know how to deal with
them.

When those people have setbacks,
when they have failures, when they are
told, "That's all wrong, you need to
do that project over," how are they
going to respond? How are they going
to know how to handle that setback,
to turn it into a transformational
learning experience from which they
can grow and continue to move
forward?

All great learning comes through
failing and making mistakes and trying
again. You have to learn how to
keep going even when you face huge

setbacks, how to just keep taking another step forward. Those of us who had so-called "learning disabilities" actually had the advantage, because we learned how to do that from a very early age. The people who were successful as children never learned those important lessons.

When children are not allowed to fail, they won't take risks. They'll be too afraid of failure to take any risks in their lives. And without taking risks, they can never reach greatness, never find their true passion or purpose and live out their mission. They will be condemned to lives of mediocrity, without the joy that comes from taking that huge step toward finding your God-given ability.

If you look at the story of any world-changer, you will notice one thing that they all have in common: they all failed in their lives. They failed faster, more frequently, and in more enormous ways than most of us can even imagine, and it is only because of those failures that they achieved their successes. Steve Jobs dropped out of college and was even fired by his own company at one point. Bill Gates, now one of the richest men in the world, quit college in his second year. Everybody said he was crazy. I say that sometimes people saying you're crazy is a good thing! It's a counterintuitive way of thinking, but that kind of thinking is what can put you a step ahead.

For many of those high school stars, that is the peak of their lives. They hit their peak at age eighteen and they get stuck because they are so afraid of failing. It's not their fault. They've been raised in a system, in a culture, in which success is so lauded and failure is so condemned that they are paralyzed. Perhaps worst of all, even parents tell their kids that failure is unacceptable. I can't even

imagine what my life would have been
if my parents had that attitude.
We need to teach our children—
and ourselves—that failure is a very
natural part of life, and in fact, it's
how most of us learn the best. With
every failure, I had a choice: is this
going to paralyze and defeat me? Am
I going to be stuck for the rest of my
life? Or am I going to learn from this,
go out, and try again? When people
have gone through their formative
years never taking risks, never failing,
and never trying for something more,
they don't have the experience to
say, "Okay, yes, I failed, but I can
do better next time." They never got
that gift.

To be a world changer, to live in your
greatness, you have to have the ability
to fail and learn and try again. Why
am I, who can barely read and write,
writing a book? Because I have learned
to risk. Writing a book is about the
farthest stretch from my natural

abilities that I could possibly think of doing. Putting together an e-learning course and teaching is the biggest risk I could take.

I wish I could tell my eight-year-old self that in less than fifty years, this is where I'd be. I wish he could hear me saying that all the failing, the running out of school at recess to hide down by the river so he doesn't have to go back, the trying and failing and trying again, would lead me to this place.

If you were that kid too, that kid who ran down and hid by the river, the kid who felt like you could never have the success that your peers were having, I'm here to tell you that you were given a gift. I know, because it happened to me. Being that kid is actually what brought me to where I am today. Because I was that kid, I am willing to do and be things and go places that other people aren't.

With every risk, with every failure, I
learned and became a better person.
As a result, I've continued to risk, to
fail, to risk again, to learn, to grow,
and to find my true place in the world.
What some people would consider a
disability, I have come to see in a new
way: I have come to see it as a gift.

CHAPTER SEVEN

Why Dyslexia's a Gift, Even if You Never Saw it That Way

This may sound completely counterintuitive, but I will be forever thankful that I was born a dyslexic. It has given me so much richness in my life. It's a strange thing to say, but it's true: All that is good about me and all that I've been able to do has a direct connection to my dyslexia. Dyslexia can seem like a curse. It can seem like it completely takes you out of this life. I felt those things so strongly that I became deeply depressed by my dyslexia. Now I view it as a great gift. It has taught me so much about myself.

The first aspect of dyslexia that makes it a gift is what we discussed in the last chapter: it gives you the ability to learn from failure, to step back and get through it and grow. The second gift dyslexia gives you is that it forces you to go to your strength. When you are dyslexic, your weakness is so severe that if you stay in it, over time it will lead you to a really bad place. It therefore forces you, from a young age, to see that you cannot survive in your weakness. Instead, you see that you have to focus on your strength—even if you don't know yet what your strength is. You see that you have to focus on what you can learn, and on the gifts and abilities that you do have.

I saw very early in my life that it was much better to focus 80 percent of my time, and effort on the things that were there, instead of living in frustration. Most people don't have this realization until much later in life. But when you are dyslexic, you are faced with difficulties in the formative years of your life, and you are forced to find your strength. You are forced to make some really hard decisions.

These decisions, as difficult as they may be, are the decisions that lead to greatness. It is only by making these difficult decisions that you begin to find the areas in which you have genius, that you are passionate about, that you love. You start finding the things that come naturally to you, that are innate to who you are. And you start building a life around those things, a foundation based on your God-given ability. You can build a great future. You can make a world-changing difference.

This doesn't mean the process is easy. In fact, it can be incredibly rough. I can remember having conversations with myself in which I said, "I can't do this, I can't do that, I can't do this other thing, what can I do?" I've had to look at myself, I've had to have the honest conversation with myself about my weaknesses and strengths. I've had to own it.

This is a very difficult thing to be faced with at a young age. You're trying to make an adult decision when you are still only a child—and that is part of the gift. The gift is that we are not wasting a whole life trying to discover who we are. In a way, that has already been predetermined. We know that we are not these ninety-nine other things, so we can work on finding the thing that we truly are.

I meet and talk to people all the time who are still wondering what their gift is. I had dinner with a couple recently, and the whole conversation was about their careers. And it was so clear to me, from the way they talked, that those careers were not what they were supposed to be doing. They are my age, and they are still struggling to find their place. There are plenty of things that they are good at, but they have not found their true God-given abilities. They have not found fulfillment. They were sitting at dinner, saying, "I'm a really good accountant, but I'm also really good at social media, and I'm also really good at recruiting, I could do HR work ..." Here they were, wonderful people, but at fifty-five years old they still didn't know what their gifts were. I can't even imagine how frustrating that would be!

People dabble for five years here, seven years there, two years at this company doing this, three years at that company doing that, and they never really find their stride. When you are forced to confront your weakness at such a young age, it pushes you to find what truly gives you fulfillment. You can't just push it down the road. You have to address it.

I didn't truly value my dyslexia as a gift until I was about forty years old. It felt like such a shame, such an embarrassment. It was so awkward at times. It was embarrassing to start a new job, to have my employer say, "Here's your computer, start calling on clients," and not be able to do it. It was embarrassing to have to look over someone else's shoulder for two weeks in order to learn how to operate a program or place an order, because I could never learn how to type.

Now I've found something that I can do, that people receive great value from, and I feel really good when I do it. I get energy from it. Now I can see it for what it is: the best thing for me. Now, at age fifty-five, I realize that I am truly blessed. I'm not sitting at dinner, thinking about all the things I'm good at, and feeling unfulfilled by all of them.

In addition to this great gift, there are actually abilities dyslexia itself gives you. Thanks to my dyslexia, I've always had an innate ability to see patterns and trends. It even extends to home decoration—I helped my mom pick out flooring and colors for the 125-year-old house she is renovating. The designer was showing us various options, and I could just see in my mind how they were going to look.

My dyslexia has also made me very sensitive to people's unspoken feelings. I can sense it in a room. If somebody is having a tough time, if somebody is struggling, if somebody is very excited about something, I can sense it. I have the ability to read people and connect with them.

These abilities come from the different focus dyslexia gives me. I am attuned to different things in the world than most people. Because I look at things so differently, I can often take an idea that other people have hashed over thoroughly and add something new to it. I always see how it can be better, because I have had to look at things differently my whole life.

My dyslexia means I put things in a different order than anyone else. I combine elements that no one else would combine, and I see patterns that no one else sees. The dyslexic brain does that, and as a result, I can see ideas, options, and ways to make things work.

I have to use my right brain and think creatively all the time. My creative, right-brain muscle has had to make up for the fact that my left-brain muscle is so weak. I've spent fifty-five years working on that one muscle, so it has become very strong.

The difficulties haven't gone away. I still get disoriented. I still have bad days. I'll have days when I mix up my schedule, when I'll leave dozens of words out of important e-mails— days when I just can't get things right. And when that happens, I have to make a choice. Just the other day I was having an incredibly rough time. I was disoriented and discombobulated. I had a presentation to do and I felt like I couldn't get myself together. But I made a choice, and I did the presentation. And when I did, the feedback was completely positive, and I was reminded that I was truly working with my God-given ability, that I had something to contribute. It brought me back to the strength of who I am.

I almost didn't write this book because I didn't have confidence in myself. I kept hearing my first-grade teacher's voice in my head: "Scott will never read. Scott will never write." It's a battle that I'm still fighting.

All these things would set me back, but I kept building on my strengths. I continued to structure my whole life around my strengths. Any task that doesn't fall within my strengths, I delegate to others. I'm incredibly lucky in that I married a woman who is brilliant and who can do many things that I cannot. She has been one of the people in my life who has helped fill in the gaps.

I am the biggest promoter of other people's talents that you will ever meet. I have twenty-one people on my team right now who all have different strengths, who all do different things, who are all geniuses. By doing this, I can focus on my strengths, they can focus on theirs, and together we can all be successful and fulfilled.

We all have a struggle. Out of that struggle, we gain a wonderful gift that we can give to the world. But until you talk about it, until you embrace your struggle and let it be a part of you, you cannot fully live in your ability. By talking about your struggle, you can connect with others. You can say, "I know exactly how you are feeling. That happened to me in school; that happened to me at work. I failed a hundred thousand times." You can start to build a community, and you no longer have to be alone. You no longer carry guilt and shame. You can be open about who you are, instead of fearing that somebody will find out you are dyslexic.

I can't tell you how many people I've encountered who, when I've asked them, "Are you dyslexic?" have gone bright red and said, "Oh my God, you found out. I'm out of a job now." And I tell them, "No, I'm excited! This is great! Now I can find you a place where you can use your gifts and abilities."

In my view, being dyslexic should be the first thing on your resume, not a shameful secret. I know that sounds way out there, but that is how things should be. I say that instead of denying it or trying to get rid of it, instead of trying to fix or change it, you should embrace it. Don't be ashamed of it, don't deny it, and don't pretend to be something that you are not. That will never work. That's what sends people to prison or into depression: living in denial of who you really are.

So many millions of people out there don't know who they are. So many people with disabilities try to hide or fix that part of themselves instead of embracing who they are and being all they can be. But once you start accepting that your disability is a blessing and a gift, once you start embracing it instead of trying to change it, you can start to find and live in your true God-given ability.

I am not trying to change who I am anymore. It may sound small, but for someone with dyslexia, that is a huge step forward. Everybody wants to take a pill or get treatment, to find a cure. But I can tell you, the best thing I ever did was to come out and tell people, "This is who I am."

This is not an easy step to take. There is so much focus in our society on "overcoming" disabilities. Differences like dyslexia are treated as something negative, something to get rid of, to deny, to overcome. People with learning difficulties get very little encouragement to be who we are, to focus on the upsides, on our strengths, rather than on what we can't fix or change.

Everybody has something to contribute, something to feel good about, something to give their lives to. All the people in jail, all the people struggling in the wrong occupations because they believe there are no other options— I want all of you to know that you have a gift. You've been told that you are never going to amount to anything, that you are going to be a janitor or a garbage collector. In truth, you could be the greatest architect of our generation. But if nobody has ever helped you believe in your abilities, you may be going home at night and drawing these beautiful plans on a sketchpad, and nobody will ever see them.

Today, great enhancements have been made in the educational system to support children with learning disabilities. But out in the working world, the support structure isn't there, and many people end up struggling. They don't have the confidence in themselves to embrace their own gifts and abilities; to embrace the blessing in disguise that their "disability" has given them.

I am here to tell you that I believe in you. Don't let anybody tell you that you aren't worth it, that you don't have any abilities. You have within you a true gift, and that is worth everything. And when you start thinking of your disability as a gift, it changes the way you feel about yourself. You begin to have confidence in yourself and your ability. Without that confidence, you can't do anything. I know, because I've lived it. I have lived without that confidence, and I have lived with it. If you have that confidence, you can face anything. The impossible becomes possible.

CHAPTER EIGHT

The World Is Going Right Brain (Even Though We Got There First)

Our whole economy has been built on the left brain. It's focused on manufacturing and the service industry, and has been for the last hundred years. But now things are starting to change. We are starting to move toward an economy of ideas. Now what is most valued is creativity—creating experiences, creating new ideas that can enhance current ideas—and that is right-brained thinking. It's not about two plus two equals four anymore. Now it's about two plus two equals seventeen.

Going forward, the people of greatest value are the people who can think like that, who can see the pattern going forward, who can imagine. That is the future. The right side of your brain is the side that thinks differently, that thinks creatively, that thinks outside the box. The right side of your brain is also the artistic side of your brain, the experience side of your brain, the visual side of your brain.

Much of the way I understand concepts is visual. When you put someone like me in a situation where all the learning is left-brained learning, or into a business situation where everything is left brain, I can't get very far. If you hand me three hundred pages of numbers, all I can say is, "Well, I guess we can recycle this." I just have no way to process that kind of information. It's all left brain. However, if somebody gave me a hundred pages of different pictures representing the idea, I would be the first to understand it. I would be the first one to tell you what it represents, what the value is, and whether the idea works or not.

So many of the very basic left-brained things we worry about are now done by computers, by microchip. The left-brained person is becoming obsolete. This is terrifying for the many people who have staked their lives on left-brained thinking. But for someone who's lived in their right brain their whole life, it's incredibly exciting. The number of opportunities that are opening up for the next generation of right-brained people is off the charts. And the people who fear becoming obsolete just need to change their way of thinking. They need to create. They need to start thinking outside the box in order to see how they can make things even better.

This shift is already starting to happen in the educational system. Many years ago, in the mid-eighties (when I was in my mid-twenties), I heard a man speak at a seminar, and he said a very interesting thing. He said, "My grandkids will not know school like you or I have all known school, where you go to a brick-and-mortar building and you sit down, and a teacher stands in front of the class. When our grandkids are in school, the schooling will be customized for each of them, broadcast from satellites onto a screen wherever they happen to be. School will be virtual, and it will be tailored for the way each individual student learns."

There were a lot of teachers at this conference, and most of them dismissed the guy. "This is just another one of those crazy futuristic people," they said. But now my niece and her husband both have teaching careers in a virtual school, and they've taught kids all over the world. My kids are adults now, and I doubt that my grandkids will ever walk into a brick-and-mortar school. They're obsolete. They don't work, because they don't teach in the way that kids learn best. Why would I risk my kids not learning in the best way they can in order to have the best possible future?

Across the globe, online learning is flourishing. The great educational institutions of the past are becoming obsolete. They are experiencing creative destruction at a rate that's hard to comprehend, and if they don't evolve, they will die. Thankfully, they are full of very smart people who will figure out how to evolve education for the next generation.

The obstacles I had to overcome as a schoolchild will be greatly diminished in the next generation. Moreover, there's so much access to information

now—information my parents didn't
have when I was a kid. The solutions
themselves are becoming less and
less expensive as well. Now a kid who
is diagnosed with dyslexia doesn't
have to have the wretched school
experience that I had.

When I think about all the
opportunities that kid is going to
have, and when I think about the
contribution that kid is going to make
to the world, I get incredibly excited.
How much creativity and value is going
to be saved that would have been lost
if we didn't embrace it?

We want to be there. We want to
be there and support these kids.
We want to encourage people to
look at education in a new and
different way, to look at education
on an individual basis. The practice
of taking five hundred kids and trying
to teach them one thing, one way is
completely outdated. It's disturbing

that we are still spending hundreds of millions of dollars to fund educational institutions that are still following that practice.

The educational system has to step up. Teachers have one of the most difficult jobs in the world, and I love them. But the system they are in does not support the kind of individual learning that is necessary for kids to be their best.

For so long, schools have emphasized left-brained things, as though those were the only things that are important, while right-brained things have been given the short stick. But art— visual arts, music, the performing arts— engages the parts of the brain that are used for creative thinking. The fact that so many institutions still insist that those areas are not important is mind-boggling. These institutions are invested in their own way of thinking. So many of them say,

"You have to have an open mind."
But they don't have an open mind to
anything that isn't left-brained. It
scares them.

But the world is finally changing.
Although many institutions seem to be
fighting against the right-brain tide—
schools are cutting the arts programs
that exercise kids' right brains—
they're fighting a losing battle. The
evidence is mounting, coming in like
a tidal wave to flood the world. And
you need to embrace it, to ride that
wave, or you'll get left behind.

Even in the typically left-brained
fields things are changing. Economics,
the sciences, math—today, you need
a right brain more and more in those
fields, too. Now it's about being
able to see how you can merge two
companies, two cultures, together into
something greater. That is a right-
brain function. Now we're a global
economy, and you have to be able to

collaborate. You have to be able to say, "Your company is in India, ours is in the United States, and together we can create something of even more value to our customers." That too is a right-brain function. So if you don't have some right-brained thinkers in your firm, you are going to be left behind.

I love collaboration. It's the future of the world. In my little company, we have people from three different continents. I've been to twenty-three countries this year alone. Everything's connected now. I'm huge on connecting people together as teams to create something new, something amazing. To me, it doesn't even feel like work—it feels like going on recess as an adult!

Businesses change more quickly than educational institutions because they are being judged by the customer every day. If the customer isn't getting greater value, if the customer isn't having a greater experience, the customer will vote with their money and go somewhere else. Not changing and adapting in business means quick death. It happens all the time. Businesses that have been around for a hundred years suddenly close down—like Kodak, for example. Kodak was brilliant at inventing over the years, but once it became solely a manufacturing company, they stopped creating value, and have since disappeared. It happens all over the place. It will be interesting, twenty to thirty years from now, to see what institutions are able to adapt and change, and which are no longer around.

The future is going to come from us right-brained people. This change is amazing for me to witness at my age. For so many years I was told, "You can't fit in. You can't do it that way. You're not going to get a job at a left-brained company. There's no future for you. There is only one way." Now, those people are sitting in their glorious towers saying, "Uh oh. What do we do now?" Now they need to hire someone with a right brain.

Some people look at me in amazement, saying, "You are always so excited about this stuff!" And it's true. I am excited, because we don't have to do this—we get to do this. This is a gift. And if it starts feeling like work, then you need to find a way to recharge your passion.

We always want to be thinking that we are the lucky ones. That kind of thinking shows up in your work. It shows up in your creativity, in the way you think about things. It shows up in the value you create for people every day. That's what separates you from everybody else: your God-given ability. Celebrate it. Live it.

CHAPTER NINE

Why My Next 55 Years Will Be Even Better Than the Last 55 Years

With the world moving rapidly toward right-brain thinking, the future is looking brighter than ever. I see opportunity in the change that is taking place across the globe. It is so different from how it was ten, twenty, thirty, or forty years ago. Now the way I naturally, instinctively think and do things is considered the best way to do them. My best skills are all on the cutting edge.

When I say that my next fifty-five years are going to be even better than the last, I don't say it glibly or irrationally. I don't say it out of left field. I say it because the indicators are there. All the trends are moving in my direction. I'm like a surfer, and I've caught the perfect wave. The world has changed, and people like me, people who think differently, are the future.

For so long, I was a square peg in a round hole. For years and years, not just in school but in the workplace, I was an odd fit. Now I am the fit. My right-brain thinking is what everybody is looking for. I read all these books, I see all this information, I go to all these seminars, I listen to brilliant people, and they are all talking about the same thing: the right brain. That's where the creativity is, that's where the value is. Companies are spending huge amounts of money to bring in right-brain talent.

When you realize that you have talents and abilities and embrace those talents and abilities, when you start to see them create value for people and make a difference in the world, and when you start to see the world moving toward the things that are inherently inside you, it's incredibly exciting. More and more people are looking for what we have. The world is finally getting on the same page as us. We are being celebrated. The way I've lived my life for the past fifty-five years is the future. And that is exciting. The world is coming to us instead of us trying to chase the world.

This is just one reason why I'm so excited for my next fifty-five years. Another reason is that fifty-five years from now, I will have experienced more change than even my grandmother, who in her early life was on a wagon train, and who was able to fly around the world before

she died. I am going to see ten
times more than she did.

The other reason is because I just
turned fifty-five, and I know I'm
only at the half-way point. When I
celebrated my birthday, I told my kids,
"I'm halfway to 110 years old, and I'm
really excited to be at halftime." I'm
super stoked for the second half of my
life. The best is ahead for me.
For so many of the valedictorians and
prom queens we discussed earlier, the
best years of their lives are behind
them. I say the best of our lives is
ahead of us. It doesn't matter where
you are or what you are doing. You
can still do more and you still have so
much more to do.

So many people in my age bracket,
from forty to sixty, are looking just to
survive the next ten, twenty, thirty,
or forty years. If you study history,
however, and if you look at the people
who have made a great impact on the

world, most of them didn't hit their stride until they were fifty. I feel that way. I understand that the wisdom, knowledge, and experience I have gathered at this point in my life has tremendous value. Now I just have to find a way to share that with the world. I want to help people discover their own value, to encourage them to have the guts to find it.

Recently I was talking to my brother, who just turned fifty. He was telling me about all the things he felt haven't worked out in his life. I stopped him and said, "Hey, this is just halftime. It's not over." My brother was a big athlete in high school, and I asked him, "How many games did you play that you won in the second half?"

"Almost all of them," my brother replied.

"Well," I said, "that's where you are now. You're in the second half."

There are many people out there who feel like they haven't accomplished what they wanted to accomplish. So many people say, "I'm fifty years old, and I'm not where I want to be. I guess I've failed in life." That's just not true. They haven't failed. They're only fifty years old—they still have decades of life to live!

If you are past fifty, you are just in the second half of your life. Any bad experiences you had in the first half, you can learn from them. You can make the second half of your life an amazing experience. As my father always used to say before he passed, "Finish strong."

So many people feel that if you haven't found your stride by a certain age, then you've wasted your life. I've encountered people who have felt that way as young as thirty-two. I had a client recently who was thirty-two years old, and he felt like a total failure. He felt like his life was over because of the failures he'd had in his twenties. When he first said that, I hardly knew what to say. "You're not even shaving yet!" I wanted to say. "Don't you realize how old I am?"

All this client would talk about was what had gone wrong. He talked about the offers he'd missed out on, the mistakes he had made. "You are only focusing on what went wrong," I pointed out.

"That's all I can think about," he said. "I can barely get up in the morning."

"You need to focus on all the wisdom you've acquired, and all you've learned from those experiences," I told him.

This kind of thinking is not at all unusual. I see it all the time. And the first thing I do is have people talk about their setbacks and mistakes.

And for each one, I ask, "What have you learned from that?" I will ask my clients to tell me about their biggest botches of the last year, the last five years, the last ten years. And then I ask them to tell me three things they learned from each experience, and how they can apply those lessons to their lives going forward, not just for themselves, but for their co-workers, their employees, their families, and their friends.

Often my clients will look at me and say, "What? It was just a terrible experience. It happened three years ago and I'm still depressed by it."

I understand that it was terrible. I've had a ton of terrible experiences in my life, so I completely understand. But you need to learn from those experiences. One of the biggest things we miss in the western world today is the great wisdom that comes out of mistakes, failures, mishaps, fears— the things that you've totally botched or done wrong. We forget to extract the wisdom. We forget to say, "Okay, I won't do that again because I know if I go there or make that choice, this is what's going to happen." All we focus on is, "I made a bad decision."

Instead, we have to ask, "What did I learn? How does it make me better? What did it teach me? Have I shared this with anybody else so that they won't make this same mistake, so they don't make this choice and have this experience?"

Your mind is brilliant. You can extract the wisdom out of your experiences. You can force yourself to think of at least one thing that you've learned, that you can apply to your life. Once you've found that wisdom, you should share it with other people. If we all shared the wisdom we've gained from our bad experiences, imagine how many of those bad experiences could be avoided!

Unfortunately, in our culture, all we want to do is talk about how bad we feel, to have a pity party. We live in a victim culture. Being a victim is celebrated, which to me is just crazy. I don't think our country was founded on that. It was founded on making your own way, being your own hero, and figuring it out. I don't believe in playing the victim card. It drives me crazy. After all, nobody has a better right to be a victim than I do. I can turn victim on and be the best victim you've ever met. I'm disabled. I was treated unfairly by the educational system. I was bullied, I was discriminated against, I was shunned, I was diagnosed as mentally challenged. I was told I would never amount to anything. I am the ultimate victim.

So why didn't I play the victim card? Because I chose not to. I chose to say, "I'm going to be my own hero. If nothing else, I'm going to believe that God made me for something. It's not going to be easy. It's not going to be simple. There are going to be many challenges, barriers, and roadblocks. But that's what I'm going to do."

And now, fifty-five years later, I'm writing a book— something I never thought I would be able to do. Now, when I see the teachers, the doctors, the psychologists who told me that I would never do anything, I can show them how far I've come by refusing to be a victim, and instead being my own hero.

You have to look toward the future instead of dwelling on the past. You cannot change the past. You can't do anything about what happened. The only thing you can do is learn from it, gather wisdom to help and guide you in the future, and to help and guide other people with the knowledge you gain.

Growing older is two sided. On the one hand, you don't have all the time in the world, so now is the time to start living intentionally, finding your purpose, and following your God-given ability. On the other hand, it's never too late to do that. There is no point in your life where it's too late. I may be ninety-seven when I create the thing that lastingly affects the world in a positive way, and I'm okay with that. Because I believe I'm going to win, even up until then.

It doesn't matter how old you are. You can still dream. You can still find your purpose, your mission, your legacy. What are you going to leave behind? Now is the time when you get to figure it out. You can become more intentional, more focused. What are you doing today that will be your legacy fifty years from now? What can you leave that will have an impact and change the world?

That's the way you have to live. For most people, most days are just routine, not too exciting. I challenge us all to take an inventory every day and ask, "Did I intentionally build toward a legacy? Did I intentionally do three things today that will carry me forward, that will help me finish strong?" Every time you do that, you build unseen momentum toward your next fifty years. Your momentum can work either for you or against you— and you have control over that.

It can be hard to look fifty years into the future, or even fifteen years into the future, or even five years into the future. It can sometimes be hard to look a week into the future. And that's fine. When that happens, you can choose today. Today, decide to be your own hero.

CHAPTER TEN

Your Future Starts Tomorrow ... So What Are You Doing with Today?

Trying to think about the next fifty years of your life can be intimidating. And the truth is, you don't have to do that. You can start with today. Where your life is going to be five, ten, or twenty years from now can be determined by the choices you make today.

So many people put off making changes in their lives. They say, "I'll do it tomorrow. I'll start making those changes tomorrow." But people only say that because they are afraid. Their minds are controlled by fear, not faith. At all times, your mind is holding on to one of those two things: fear or faith. Twenty-four/seven, 365, for as long as you are breathing, one or the other is going to be in your mind—either fear or faith. You get to choose which. You have to ask yourself, are you living and waiting to die, or are you living to live? I ask this question of people all the time. If we are just living waiting to die, we are living in fear.

In order to start moving from fear into faith, you have to start at the lowest level. It has to be the simplest thing. For somebody who is fear-ridden, the first step has to be something non-threatening. If it's too big, there is too much fear to overcome, and you can't get through to the actions of faith.

I worked with a client who was
completely paralyzed by fear, and
their first step was simply going for a
walk for twenty minutes during lunch
instead of just sitting in the lunch
room and gossiping for an hour. It
was just that, that one tiny step. It
all started with that twenty-minute
walk during lunch to avoid gossiping.
She had realized that the gossip was
creating major fear in her life every
day, with everybody talking about
layoffs, about who was going to
have to move, about whether or not
they were going to get a bonus. She
realized it was feeding her fear, so
she decided just to leave for twenty
minutes a day.

From that first step, it was amazing
how quickly she moved on to some
pretty significant steps of faith,
and stepped out of fear. In order
to make those steps, we had to
start somewhere that my client was
comfortable. And within a week, she

was ready to add more and more things. She started to say, "I can do this." That is the unseen momentum of faith that starts building. Now this client is starting to share that momentum with her team at work. Now she is not a person whom you would ever think lived in fear in any way.

The first step into faith is different for every person. It all depends on where you are. Every person is at a different place in a different scenario. You just have to figure out what that step is for you. It's okay to slow down. This is not the Internet; it's your life. It doesn't go at 150 MB a minute. No step is too small. That's how you build confidence. Remember that anything that starts today, anything you do, even one tiny baby step, is something to be celebrated. It doesn't matter what it looks like, or how small it is. We are going to document it, we are going to celebrate it, we are going to tell people about it, and we are going to become stronger because of it.

I lived my whole childhood going from baby step to baby step. I just took one step at a time, and by the time I was done with school, I found that I could run a marathon. It was only by starting to take small steps that I've found myself where I am today: writing a book, creating an e-learning course, coaching business owners, speaking to crowds of 10,000 people, and doing the things that I was always told I could never do. My greatest fear for so many years has now become part of my legacy and my contribution to the world.

All that starts with today. What are you doing differently right now so that you can live the best today that you possibly can? I'm not talking about climbing Mount Everest today. I'm talking about doing one or two things that will make today a day full of life.

I'm talking about choosing to live in faith rather than fear.

It doesn't have to be huge and intimidating. You can just think about two or three things that you can do today. You don't have to have a fifty-year plan, or even a five-year plan. You just have to have a plan for today. That's how you start making changes in your life and in the world: not by saying, "In the next thirty years, I have to do this," but by saying, "Today, I'm going to do this."

This kind of thinking is like a muscle. A few months ago my wife signed me up for this crazy boot camp thing. It was just torture. By the fourth day of the first week, I was so sore I could not bend over to get into my car. I thought I was in shape. I used to play sports. I thought I was in pretty good condition. It turns out, I was not! But now, after several months of this boot camp four or five times a week, those muscles have developed. Now I can do boot camp in the morning and go for a two-hour bike ride in the evening!

This is exactly the same process you can use to build your legacy, to live out your God-given mission. By doing just one or two or three things a day, you build up that muscle. And don't just do it—record it. Document it. Write it down. There's something that happens when we actually write down a goal, an achievement, or an accomplishment. It may be as simple as sending a note to your loved ones saying, "Hey, I've been thinking about you. I love you." When you have that log of what you've done, of the steps you've taken, you can start to really feel what you've achieved. You can actually read the story of your legacy.

Make writing down those two or three things the last thing you do before you go to sleep at night. I guarantee you that three months later, six months later, a year later, three years later, that is not going to be a sore, weak, fragile, fear-filled muscle. Your life is going to be full of faith and belief in your legacy, your future, and how you can change the world— because you are changing the world already by changing yourself.

The power of doing this right before you go to sleep is that your subconscious mind— your heart, your body, your soul— has the last input of the day. All night while you are sleeping, your mind, your supercomputer, will be building you up.

Six months down the road, you will find that when you get upset, when you start thinking, "I haven't gotten much done," your mind will automatically say, "No, do you remember, you did this today. This happened, and you're able to do that." Pretty soon, you'll realize that you are really starting to get going. You'll start feeling like you are really living with tremendous purpose in your life. Your mind will not be controlled by fear anymore, but by faith. That will start to give you the courage and confidence to do things you never thought possible.

All you have to do is make the commitment and stick to it. Just do two or three things a day, and never go to sleep without writing them down. I never put my head on the pillow without writing down the things that I am grateful for and that I have achieved that day.

With this simple exercise, you will become the Arnold Schwarzenegger of faith. When people ask me how I can be so confident, so encouraging, so willing to take risks, I tell them it is because I have built up that muscle that enables me to live in faith instead of fear. I don't feed fear anymore; I feed faith. I feed that belief, that confidence, that trust that I do have a mission, that I do have God-given abilities, that I do have a God-given purpose, that I can change the world, and that I can change the world by changing myself.

However, this only works if you are willing to take that first step. It only works if you are willing to say, "I did it. I seized the day. I took half a step. I can celebrate that. I am going to focus my thoughts and energy on the fact that I did this." If we all do this every day, if we all live this way and share it with the people in our lives, the world will be changed.

Making a huge life change, a huge change in thinking, can seem like an impossible challenge. Becoming your best self can seem so far away. But the truth is, you are great right now. You are great because you are taking the small steps. You are great today. By taking those small steps, you feed your faith, you feed your confidence, and you create your legacy. By taking those small steps, you are developing the courage to make a change. How do you make yourself get into freezing cold water? One step at a time. All I want you to do is just get your toe in the water by starting now. Start today. Do something. Start making a change. You can do one simple thing, right now, and start changing your experience, your contribution, and your world.

The future is not far away, out of reach. It starts right now. The future is today; the dream is today. The real treasure is the process, not the destination. The process of discovering that dyslexia is my greatest advantage has been a true gift. That process has taken fifty-five years, and it has been amazing.

Today is the time to take inventory of your advantage, of your unique, God-given ability to change the world, an ability that is completely unlike what anybody else has. We're all unique. We're all different. No matter what age you are, this is the prime of your life. This is when your legacy is written. It's not ten years from now; it's today. Today is the time to seize it, to live it out.

Today is all we have. Today matters. Today is your legacy fifty years from now. Today is it. This is not a dress rehearsal; this is the production of your life right now. There are no do-overs. You don't get a do-over of today.

There is no better time to do this than now. Tomorrow's not going to be a better day. Ten years from now is not going to be a better time. You're in the best place in your life to do this, right now, today. You have everything you need to start. Whatever it is, whatever the step is for you, you have everything you need to take it.

If you have a learning disability, if you are struggling, if you are feeling discouraged, depressed, defeated, or full of fear, I'm here to tell you that today matters, and that you can start changing all of that today, with just one little step.

CHAPTER ELEVEN

What Are Your God-Given Ability, God-Given Purpose, and God-Given Mission? And How Can You Live Them Out in Your Life Today?

Most people become motivated to start living in their God-given ability when they reach a certain level of frustration or discontent. Eventually you get to a point where you have to get serious about figuring out what you are supposed to be doing in your life, what your gifts are, what your passion and purpose are. When you get to that point, you can start being honest with yourself— not with anyone else, but with yourself. You can start to say, "This is not working. This is not who I am." If you are not putting your head on your pillow at night with a great sense of content and purpose, if you are struggling, then it's time to start asking questions.

It all starts with being honest and saying, "I'm not happy. I'm not doing what I was made to do. I am just trudging through life, and I am not finding that meaning that I want to find." You cannot find that meaning if you are not being and doing what you were made to do.

Eighty percent of people in the world are going to a job, a career, an occupation, that isn't really connected to their God-given ability. It's no wonder that there is so much domestic unhappiness in the world. I believe a large part of it is that people are so frustrated at work. When you spend so much time doing something that you are frustrated or bored with, that you couldn't care less about, it makes a difference. And when you then have to spend an hour commuting home in traffic, and then your car breaks down ... By the time you walk in the door, it's no wonder that you are unhappy.

Imagine what our economy would be, what our world would be, if the percentages were flipped, if 80 percent of people were working in occupations that utilized their God-given abilities? Imagine waking up in the morning and saying, "I've got a full day of doing the type of thing I love," instead of rolling out of bed and saying, "Okay, I have to do this, this, and this, and then maybe at 5:15 I'll be able to do something I'm excited about." Imagine the change that would make in our lives, in our world. It would be amazing.

Making that change in your own life takes great strength and courage. It means being willing to admit, "I've been miserable doing this for all these years." That is incredibly difficult. It's hard to be that honest. We have parents and co-workers and bosses and siblings and spouses and partners and friends all saying to us, "You have a degree in this area; you have to do this! It would be such a waste if you didn't." Or, "You've been at this company for seventeen years; you can't change now." We hear this from the people around us, we think it ourselves, and we get paralyzed. We get stuck.

I was told when I was young that I could only be one thing: a janitor. For someone like me, who is social and completely people-driven, who operates the way I operate, that was like a death sentence. I was going to have to clean toilets, mop floors, and be completely alone. It was the worst thing I could imagine.

We get stuck because we are not listening to our hearts. We are not being honest. That is why I am screaming from the highest mountain that you don't have to accept what you're told by other people tell that you have to be. Instead, you have to trust what you know about yourself that other people may not know.

You need to look at your life and take inventory of the things you've done that have brought you joy. Think of the things you've done that may have been work for other people, that were challenging for other people, that were drudgery for other people, but that you were energized by, that made you come alive. You want to find that thing for which your passion just grows when you do it. You want to find that thing you don't grow weary of.

You have to take the time and effort to ask yourself, in all honesty, what are the experiences that make you really come alive? If you think back through your whole life, what have you done that made people say, "You really have a knack for that"? Think of the things that come easily to you, that you do well, that you have a talent for. Think back to times when you have felt that you were in a groove. Those are all indicators, signposts guiding you toward your God-given ability.

Once you start identifying your God-given ability, you need to start to keep track of how much time you spend enjoying those abilities. Most people find that 80 percent of their lives are spent doing things that are not related to their God-given abilities, that they don't find purpose in, that they are not passionate about. Because of that, they don't have meaning at the end of the day, at the end of the year, or at the end of their lives.

The next step in the process is figuring out how to rearrange your life so that 80 percent, 70 percent, or even just 50 percent of your life is spent doing those activities that are your **God-given ability.**

Even if you innately know where you should be, it can be very hard to convince yourself that you can actually do it, that you can actually live and make a living doing it, that you can truly have that purpose in your life. For most people, it is not logistically possible to drop everything and run off in a new direction. But just because you can't quit your job today and find a new job tomorrow doesn't mean you can't start taking the steps to find the thing you love, to start participating in it.

Depending on where you are in your life, this can take some time. If you are in a career, if you have responsibility to a marriage, or if you have family obligations, you can't just jump ship. Even if you realize that 80 percent of your job does not fit your God-given ability, you can't just say, "Tomorrow I'm going to go be a character at Disneyland because that's what I'm really passionate about!" Realistically speaking, it can't be that sudden.

However, you can take steps toward that goal. You can stay at your job and start getting involved in local theater. You can start to have some part of your life in which you are actually doing what you are passionate about. Just that small step will help you start to discover who you are, which will help you to find yourself again.

I have a client who has been at a company for thirty-two years and is miserable. He's successful in this company, and he's never worked anywhere else in his life, but he is

gasping for air. Even though his is
uncomfortable, he is paralyzed by his
perceived security in this job. He's
caught up in the little distractions—
the paid vacation, the benefits, the
retirement. So I told him, "Let's just
start with one thing. Let's look at
something that doesn't have anything
to do with those little distractions.
Try volunteering one day a month,
doing something you feel like you are
passionate about." Even this step
was hard for him to take. He was
so caught up in the corporate thing
for thirty-two years that now it was
taking him a very long time to make
this first step.

The transition is going to be painful.
The change is going to be hard. But
at the end, if you get to live 60 to
70 percent of your life doing what
you are passionate about, it's worth
it. I had another client who worked
in a job that was just grinding her
down. For a long time, she could not

find anything that gave her purpose or meaning. I asked her when was the last time she had felt in the zone, and happy with what she was doing. She started talking about working with younger children, about how she used to volunteer at her kids' school, and about how before she was married she would volunteer in classrooms and at the library.

"Well," I said, "let's start there. Let's start making a path. Let's take one step back toward that."

When I said that, when we started talking about it as a real possibility, I could see the transformation already starting in her. "Do you really think I could do that?" she asked.

"Of course," I said. "Just try volunteering at the library on Saturdays. Read books to kids. And tell me what happens."

As soon as she started volunteering, she said, "Oh my gosh, I think this is where I need to be." She had been living in fear, paralyzed by her job and what it represented to her. Now she was starting to move into living in her God-given ability.

There is a great need for volunteers in our country. There are many opportunities to volunteer for three months or six months, to really test something out and see if it is the right thing for you. By volunteering, you are not distracted by the idea of a paycheck or a promotion. You are doing something because you genuinely love it. You are giving your time out of yourself, rather than being influenced by retirement benefits or three weeks of paid vacation. All of those things pull us away from our God-given abilities. They trick us into seeking security instead of seeking what we are truly passionate about.

As a volunteer, there's no benefit. They're never going to pay you. There's nothing in it for you except that it's something you think you are passionate about.

This is one of the important things to remember as you start to find your mission, your purpose, and your passion: you don't necessarily have to know what career path you want to follow. You need to get out of your mind, especially at the beginning of the process. You need to forget the idea of a job or a career or a title. Instead, you have to think of the general idea. Then, gradually, you can start to hone in on where that idea may take you.

Perhaps there was a class in, say, oceanography that you took in college when you were twenty-one. You loved the work you were doing, but your parents told you that you couldn't major in that area because it wouldn't be economically prudent. But you still think about the class all the time. Now you're an adult, and you're on your own. So why don't you start volunteering at the aquarium and see where that leads?

And if you volunteer and you find that you don't like it, that is great too! You've given a day or a few hours of your life, and you've learned something incredibly valuable. You may need to try things out— to volunteer and do things like that— for six months, for a year or two, or even for three years or five years, in order to make the transition. But when you are working toward your God-given ability, even the process is awesome. It's exciting, because you know you are working to get to where you should be.

Sometimes I encounter people who truly cannot think of a time when they were happy, of something that gives them meaning, purpose, and fulfilment.

I had a client who at age fifty-two told me that he had never been happy in his entire life. For an hour, he told me about all the unhappiness in all the different parts of his life. Fifty-two years is a long time to be unhappy!

After this client told me his story, my response seemed to be overly simple. I said, "Maybe we should focus on simply doing the opposite of what you've been doing for the past fifty-two years." Considering the sheer negativity in his work, in his family situation, and in his whole life, this was my suggestion. "If you are this unhappy," I said, "perhaps doing the opposite of everything you've ever done would put you somewhere where you could have a sense of happiness."

We had a long discussion about it, and he decided to start going at life differently. One of the first choices he made was to have a relationship with his kids again— something he hadn't done in many, many years. I asked him what that might entail, and he said, "Maybe I should send them an e-mail or call them."

"Those are your children," I said. "I think that connection might start to give you the sense of being a father again, which is something that you haven't been." This simple thing would be the opposite of what he had been doing for so long. "Why don't we start there," I said.

He told me that deep down in his heart, he really would like to be their father. Being a father myself, I know the joy of fatherhood. And that simple step—contacting his children—is where we started.

Even if you feel like you haven't found something in your life that makes you happy, if you haven't had that experience of doing something you love, of finding your groove, of practicing your ability, there is still always somewhere you can start. You can still find a way to happiness, to your purpose, to your mission.

When you are working toward your purpose, toward having meaning in your life, waking up on Monday morning ceases to be a drag and becomes exciting. You wake up and say, "Let's go do our work! Let's go contribute! Let's go do more!" You are no longer dragging yourself to work; you are running toward it!

As you start to live in your God-given ability more every day, you start to gather momentum. You start feeling like you want to do more and more. My clients tend to accelerate the process themselves. They spend three to six months starting to live in their ability, and when they come in for an appointment, I ask them how much time in the past week they spent working at their God-given ability and how much time they spend doing other things. Just within that short span of time, they'll already have jumped up to 40 percent of their time spent living in their God-given ability.

They will have figured out how somebody else can do the accounting in their business, because it really drains and stresses them. They've found somebody who has that strength and that ability, and now they are freed up to do the recruiting and training. And they will say to me, "I'm loving this! Now, I'm working on delegating these other two areas to people who have those strengths and abilities, so I can do more of this other thing that is one of my strengths."

This is part of the shift: delegating the tasks that are not among your God-given abilities. This is what I particularly recommend to business people. If there is an area that isn't your strength, in which you struggle, then you can find somebody on your team or hire somebody who does have that strength. You can find someone whose God-given ability is in that area, who is passionate about that area. You can partner with people in order to restructure your life.

That's what a company should be: a group of individual people combining their talents, their gifts, and their work in order to get a result. Consider the potential that is lost every day in these companies and organizations simply because they do not do a good job matching people up with their God-given abilities. If everybody in a company worked in their God-given ability, imagine the possibilities! We've seen it before in companies like Apple. What a company is comes down to the people, to their God-given abilities. That's what makes a company special. The more a company focuses on its people and their individual talents and abilities, the better the company will do.

I had a client who had been in a partnership for many, many years. The company was very successful. However, he and his partner had many serious negative confrontations and disagreements, over and over again through the years. Finally, just a few months ago, he realized that he needed to end that partnership. He needed to go start his own company.

The energy this change has given him is amazing. It's like talking to a different person now. He just needed to take the responsibility to remove that negativity from his life. Now he's starting a company built around his God-given ability, what he's passionate about—his mission. And now all the staff from the other company is coming to work for him!

Everyone wanted to come work for him because he told them, "I want you to do what you're great at. I want to celebrate what you're great at. I'm going to recognize you for what you are great at." He is building a whole company based on his employees' God-given abilities—and that is a place where people want to work. It's the greatest recruitment tool in the world.

Imagine if you walked into a job interview and the interviewer said, "Tell us what you are really passionate about. Tell us what your God-given abilities are. Tell us what gets you up at five o'clock in the morning to be the first in the office, and what you want to do all day, five days a week. Tell us about that." Then, when you tell them about it, they say, "Okay, we have that; we have such a position at our company." Or they say, "We don't have that position, but I have a friend who has a company, and I just talked to him at lunch the other day and they need somebody who has that gift."

I think we have the whole job thing backward. Why should a résumé just list all the jobs that weren't right for you? Why should it just show the job you trudged to and slaved at for seven years? It would be so much better if everybody had a résumé of all the things that they were really good at and really loved doing. And what if in college you spent your senior year identifying the field of study in which you could best live out your God-given abilities? It would make such a difference in the world.

This shift is already starting to happen. The next generation, the people who are coming of age now, are not just looking for a paycheck. They are looking for something meaningful, for a way they can contribute and collaborate, a way to use their genius and their God-given abilities. They are not just trying to find security. They want something that matters.

I love this new generation. My wife and I spend a lot of time with people aged eighteen to thirty. I've taken them on trips to Africa, to India, to Haiti. The new generation is honest. They stand up and say, "This is not for me." They know what they are passionate about, and they ask, "How can we work this into our lives? How can we have work that is meaningful, that we feel good about, that makes a difference?"

When people start asking those questions, and when they start to realize they can actually live in their God-given ability, they open up like flowers. They start to understand what living a meaningful life feels like. They start to realize their potential, and they realize how big the future can be. As you start living in your God-given ability, you become more confident that this is what you are supposed to be doing.

This is when your real life begins—
when you realize that your dream
really can come true. You really can
put in time working at that homeless
shelter. Sure, it will be financially
different for you and your family.
Sure, there isn't a huge guaranteed
retirement. But if you want to make a
difference and you know you are going
to feel good about what you're doing,
and if it is important to you, then it is
worth it.

What's more, once you have found
a way to live in your God-given
ability, you never have to stop—and
you shouldn't stop. When I was in
the insurance business, I learned of
a trend insurance companies are very
aware of: when men retire, many of
them die or contract a major illness
within two years of retirement. I
believe that is because these men look
back and say, "I didn't do what I was
meant to do. My life didn't really have
the meaning and purpose I thought it

would have." When you start having those thoughts at sixty-five, it's very easy to get depressed, to get discouraged. And when that happens, you become susceptible to illness.

I don't believe in retirement— not if you are working in your God-given ability. If you are really living your mission and purpose, why would that end just because you turn sixty-five? Unfortunately, many people never find that thing that makes them happy— that purpose, that mission. And then, when they retire, they have nothing left to live for.

In many cultures, when you reach a certain age, you are sought after for wisdom and knowledge. The experience of age is revered. But in our culture, that is not the case. I believe that needs to change. There are plenty of things that I know now, at fifty-five, that I did not know at thirty-five, or even forty-five. There are no shortcuts to life experience.

We are missing out on all that wisdom by putting people in homes, by forcing people to retire, by saying, "It's over, you can no longer contribute in this area." I think that's crazy. We're throwing this wonderful asset away. Why in the world would we do that? We wonder why we make so many wrong choices as a culture, and I think the answer is obvious: because we won't listen to the people who have been through it before.

Instead, we need to value the contribution that people can continue to make throughout their whole lives. I say that when you turn seventy-five, you can start thinking about what the next part of your life is going to be about. You can start thinking about what your contribution will be in this next part of your life, what your mission will be, what your purpose will be. Because your life is not over. With the technology and healthcare we have now, you could easily still be completely productive at age ninety-five. We need to stop letting other people dictate to us when our productive life is over. It's not over until you say it's over. There is still so much you can do.

No matter where you are in your life, living in your God-given ability doesn't have to be a far-off fantasy. It can start right here, right now. It can become the mission of your life. And at the end of your days, people will say, "That is what this person is about. That is what they brought to the world. This was their purpose, this was their mission, and look at the impact they made."

You can go to sleep at the end of the day thinking, This was a good day. I really did what I was meant to do. I really made a difference. I'm on my way to fulfilling the mission I want for my life. I am living in my God-given ability. All you have to do is take ownership and responsibility. All you have to do is say, "I'm not the victim anymore." Let's start that process. Let's go on that great adventure. You are in control of your destiny, and you can make the decisions and changes that you want to make.

And you can celebrate the result. It can be all that you imagined, and so much more. People shock themselves, and they say, "Wow, this is really happening!" Yes, it really happens, and it can happen for you.

CHAPTER TWELVE

What Can the Confidence Coach Do for You?

The first seeds of Confidence Coach were planted when I was in the insurance business. The insurance industry started to change, and my two partners and I were struggling. In fact, we were on the verge of losing the business. So we hired a coach. For three people who had been very successful for fifteen years, it took a lot of humble pie swallowing for each of us to say, "Well, maybe I don't know everything. Maybe I do need a coach. Maybe we need to be held accountable. Maybe we need to face some of these demons that we just keep shutting away in the closet."

For three years, we met with the coach every month. He asked really tough questions, and made us make tough choices. During this process, I fell in love with working on the business. I fell in love with the idea of being coached. I fell in love with learning from somebody who was totally detached from our business, yet willing to really make us work, to make us face the things that made us uncomfortable, to face the things we wanted to run away from.

The result of this coaching was that all three of us realized that we all wanted something different out of our lives at that point. We had run this business for eighteen years, and now we were ready to sell it. So shortly after we finished the coaching, we sold the company.

Once we sold the company, I needed to figure out what to do. I was at mid life, fifty years old. So I asked myself, "What do I want the second half of my life to be about? What legacy do I want to leave? What is meaningful to me? What are my God-given abilities?" As I spent some time searching for the answers to those questions, a number of people—business owners, CEOs, and other people who ran companies—called me and asked, "Can you meet with me and talk about what's happening in my company?"

I started doing this, meeting with these business people, just because I wanted to help people out. I never meant it to be a real business.

Then the company that had provided the coaching for my company contacted me. "We're going to have a coaching training," they told me. "You were so successful as a client; would you be interested in participating in the training?" I attended the seminar, and I fell in love with the whole idea of coaching. I went through some intensive training for a year to become a certified coach.

When I started coaching, it was like a glove fitting perfectly on my hand. It was my God-given ability. It was something I was passionate about. I started coaching for people I knew when they came to me asking for help. I didn't even realize what I was doing until my wife said, "You know, I think this is a business."

"No," I said. "I'm just helping out people I know. It's just something I enjoy doing. I don't think it's a business." But eventually I realized that it could be a business. I had something to offer, a God-given ability that I was passionate about, a service that people would want. So I started a business.

For the first time in my life, with Confidence Coach, I'm really excited to go to work on Monday morning. I'm not dragging myself out of bed, thinking, "I've got to make it to Friday." Instead, I start at five o'clock in the morning, super excited—and I am not a morning person! I regularly put in long days, and I love it.

Because of my experience with the insurance business, I can tell when a business leader, a CEO, or someone running a company is having difficulties. I can recognize it because I've been there. I know what it feels like. However, I don't look at it as a bad thing. I look at it as an opportunity to change, to turn things around ... and that is where Confidence Coach can help.

So many entrepreneurs and CEOs are excellent at working in their businesses. But there's a huge difference between working in a business and working on a business. I've heard so many people who are working in a business say, "Here I am, working harder than ever, and it's not getting any better. It's getting worse." The problem is that they are not working on their businesses.

I take my clients through a process in which they change their mindsets from only working in the business to taking three or four hours or half a day out of every month to work on the business. That means taking the time to work on the strategic part of the business, the part that may have been forgotten in the ten or twenty years since they started the business. We call this process The Gameplan™. I'm a huge sports fan, as are many CEOs, business owners and entrepreneurs, so we use that as a way to illustrate the process.

We take our clients through the idea of creating a world championship

business. We talk about putting some
of the fun back in their business and
remembering why they started in the
first place. We work on creating a
winning strategy, and I have them
write that strategy out and revisit
the roots of the company. We ask,
"How does the original mission of
this company line up with what you're
doing in business now, with the players
you have on your team? What are your
winning plays today?"

We take them through the whole game
plan, and we help them remember
that they had a vision, a dream, when
they started this company. We help
them re-connect with their roots and
rediscover the true meaning of their
business. If you are our client, we
want to help you move away from
the things that are not within your
company's mission, that are not your
team's God-given abilities. Sometimes,
the biggest step can be asking, "Why
are we doing this? We thought this
would be a good idea, but did we ever

check it against our game plan? Did
we check it with our players? Does it
really fit who we are? Do we really
believe in this? Is this something we're
passionate about?" In many cases, you
can actually add to your business by
subtracting, by getting back to your
fundamental business.

At Confidence Coach, we hold our
clients accountable throughout that
process, encouraging them to be
grateful, to track achievement, to
celebrate success. We also ask, "How
are you doing on your goals? How are
you going to approach this problem?
Are you staying true to your mission?"

Moreover, we hold you accountable
for maintaining new habits—simple
but subtle changes that affect the
momentum in your life and in your
team's lives. These new habits create
an environment that enables you to
win at your business. We can help
you keep your focus on winning, rather

than focusing all the time on what is going wrong, on what you've lost, or what product or service didn't work out. Instead, we help you always think forward to the idea of winning, and create a culture of winning in your business. Part of this process is simply stopping and saying, "Hey, look what we've achieved. Look at what we can be grateful for. Look at the contribution we have made." Take the time to celebrate every day.

Another thing we teach our business clients is how to manage time and money. If you are married, if you have a family, if you have children, whatever is in your life outside of work, we help you figure out how to encourage those parts of your life to thrive. We show you how to take back control of that life. We make sure your business begins to serve your life, your family, and your community in the way you have always envisioned that it would.

We also offer coaching on The Unfair Dyslexic Advantage™. If you're dyslexic, we teach you how to change your mindset and understand that being dyslexic is actually your greatest advantage. We help you through that self-discovery, help you find the genius within yourself, and help you find those two or three things about which you can say, "I'm in the top one percent of people in the world doing this thing!" We can help you re-negotiate your life and re-configure your time to focus on those things, and help you get rid of all the other junk that weighs you down, that frustrates you and causes anxiety, fear, and stress.

We help you build on your strengths; we don't want you to spend any more time on any of your weaknesses. We want you to spend 70 percent of every living day going forward in your strength, and we'll equip you with the tools to do that. We'll help you understand how your "disability" is something to be proud of and to celebrate.

One of the things we're working on now is organizing a Dyslexic Mastermind global community where once a year amazing dyslexic people will come together and share their victories and wisdom, and we can all celebrate together. There are so many great dyslexic minds that have accomplished so much, and there is no place for them all to come together. We want to start a movement that changes the world, that opens the conversation, that raises awareness of the gift of dyslexia.

Whether you have dyslexia or not, Confidence Coach can still help set you on a better path. Most people in the world are spending eighty percent of their time on stuff they are not really passionate about, that they are not really good at. I'm currently working with a business owner who is not dyslexic or "disabled" in any way. However, until recently he's been doing a lot of stuff that he's mediocre at, that he is not passionate about, that is pure drudgery for him. At the time he came to us, he had lost all his passion, and was stuck in the malaise of his life.

Now, we've been working together for six months, and we have been pulling all of that stuff away and getting rid of it. After several conversations, we figured out where he needed to focus, what his God-given abilities were, and we identified his God-given purpose and his God-given mission. Now he's doing what he's passionate about—working with people, working with his team, being out in the field—and he is coming alive. It's a complete transformation, and it's only been six months.

Our next step is developing a plan to encourage a similar transformation in his children. "I've never been able to figure that out," he told me.

"What is the one thing you want them to know?" I asked. "What is the legacy, memory, or feeling you want to make sure they know? Are you having those conversations with your children?" He told me that he wanted his kids simply to know he loved them. And we started to figure out what conversations he could have with his children and how he could tell them that. Now great things are happening with his son and daughter. They express their love and gratitude on a daily basis, whether on the phone or in person. Although not business related, these are the types of insights and experiences we can bring about that really make a difference for people and their families.

Our coaching is customized for each client. I've never had two clients who have been in the exact same spot. Although they may have common challenges, everyone is in a different place. Everybody has a unique experience before they come to us. We want to know about your unique experience, to respect it and develop a process based around where you are coming from and where you are going. We want to be the jet fuel that takes your specific rocket from here to the moon.

When we start our coaching sessions, for the first couple months it's really just a conversation. I ask clients where they see themselves going, what the barriers are to taking that path, and what the obstacles are in their lives right now, both in their business lives and their personal lives. I ask what they are running up against— where they stop. We'll talk about what they think their greatest advantages are, what may be their greatest opportunities, and what situations may exist that they haven't taken advantage of. And of course, we'll talk about what they are great at, what their passion is.

We will have three or four conversations on these topics. Then, depending on the client's answers, we'll figure out the fastest way to start building their confidence. We will start rebuilding your life around your God-given abilities, around the genius of who you are.

Confidence Coach is also launching an e-learning series, which can be found at http://course.confidencecoach.org/courses/the-gratitude-experience/.

We have already talked about the first course in the series, The Gratitude Experience™. This course is highly visual and highly interactive. In a video and with animation, I introduce the ideas and work through them. The need for gratitude is universal. If all I am ever known for in my life is helping people to be more grateful, I'll be ecstatic. By starting with a course on gratitude, we are starting with an audience of seven billion.

We are also offering an e-learning course on being married to or being in a relationship with a dyslexic. My wife is leading that course, covering what to be aware of and how to understand how a dyslexic person is wired. There isn't anything else like this out there, and we think it will be incredibly helpful.

Another course we are offering is on dreaming. This course is about igniting the dreams lying dormant in your soul.

We have seen over and over that for most people, motivation doesn't come from money, but from their own passions— their goals, dreams, visions, and hopes for themselves, their family, and their community. You can help your co-workers, your students, your teammates, and your family achieve those dreams, and when they do, you can celebrate it.

If you want to inspire people, if you really want to get the best out of them, you should start by asking, "What's your dream?" Try it to see what happens.

"I've always wanted to learn how to play the piano," they might say. This person may have worked for you for seven years, and you never knew that. But they know that you have a piano in your office, and that you are a very accomplished piano player who has a really great teacher. If you really want to get behind this person's dream, you'll say, "I'm going to give you a key to my office, and I'm going to pay for a year with my piano teacher."

This is actually a true story. This happened to one of my clients. She had been working at this company seven years, and her boss offered her access to the piano and piano lessons. Now, what do you think her response is when somebody asks her about her job, about her company, about her boss? She is now the best employee there could be. She is the best advertising a company could ever have, and she is as loyal as anybody will ever be. If you had given her a million dollar raise, she would not be as loyal as she is now. She is proof that the key to having a company of excited, motivated people is to have a company of people who are achieving their dreams. Rather than dragging themselves to work in the morning, they will be excited to come in, because their job is now a vehicle for them to achieve their dreams.

This doesn't just apply to the workplace. This can apply to a classroom, a sports team, or a family. No matter where you are a leader, leadership is always about serving other people's dreams. The ultimate function, the ultimate responsibility of a business owner, a **CEO**, or a manager is to make sure that the people serving with you are living out their dreams—whatever those dreams are. No dream is too small or too big. You can always help them achieve it. What's the first step toward achieving their dreams?

The ultimate responsibility of a teacher is to help children to achieve their dreams. Imagine what school would be like if on the first day, the teacher said, "Okay, we're going to start by talking about your dreams, your hopes for the future, and how this class can help you achieve them." This would be remarkable, for the students and for the teacher. It would be like the experience I had in the sixth grade with Mr. Bakala, who said, "I'm going to give you a chance to find your dream." He threw gasoline on my fire. I'm sitting here today because somebody, even if indirectly, gave me the opportunity to find my dream.

Think about how different our government would be, how different our country would be, if our politicians said, "What are the dreams of the people who live in my community, my city, my state, my country, and how can we help them get there?" It would change everything.

I am where I am today solely because I'm a dreamer. I dream to the point of scaring myself. I dream the most impossible dreams, and I believe in them—like the dream that I, the worst student in my school, would someday be teaching e-learning classes, or the dream that I would someday be financially free. I've accomplished so many of my dreams, it's staggering. I can't even keep track of them all. But the only reason I am able to do so is because I dream them in the first place.

To be a dreamer, you need to surround yourself with other dreamers. Don't let yourself be surrounded by people who are not dreamers, because they will tear you down. That is why leaders need to be dreamers— so they can support other people's dreams as well.

If you don't have dreams, you don't have hope. That is the downfall of Western civilization: the lack of dreams. People go to factories, to offices, to their jobs, as though they were robots. They have no hope for the passion in their souls.

Confidence Coach can help you find your passion. We can help you find your dreams and follow them. We want to be a dream catalyst for you. I want to share with you my energy, my joy, and my encouragement. I want to encourage you and your soul. I want you to have hope. I want you to believe that there's a purpose for you. I want you to experience all these things. Moreover, I want you to pass it on to your family, to your friends, to other entrepreneurs. It doesn't end with you. You can share your legacy with all those around you.

At Confidence Coach, we want you to go to sleep at night grateful and fulfilled. There's a song I listen to all the time called "It Is Well With My Soul." I listen to it over and over, and that is the benefit I get from living in my God-given ability, living in my passion, and living with gratitude. We want you to put your head on the pillow at night and think, *It is well with my soul.*

If you are ready to start that journey,
or if you want to learn more,
you can visit our web site at:

www.confidencecoach.org

or call us at:

1-800-768-2217

Together, we can help you achieve
your dreams, create your legacy, and
find and live in your God-given ability.

ACKNOWLEDGMENTS

We want to take a moment to thank all those who really helped what was once our vision become our reality. Our gratitude extends to...

...Christian Boer and his team, the creators of Dyslexia Font (www. dyslexiafont.com). They have created a revolutionary font, which simplifies all fonts to make it easier to read for people with dyslexia. We use the font throughout the entire book, and Christian and his team gave us valuable input on the design and layout of the text, so that our book is a unique product that makes reading fun and enjoyable for everybody, and importantly, for those with dyslexia.

...Choose Growth (www.choosegrowth. com) for their amazing creativity, collaboration and for being our e-learning partners and platform.

...Jon Eischen at GeoCatalyst (www. geocatalyst.com) for his great web design.

...Josiah Jost at Siah Design (siahdesign.com) for his original design concepts for our coaching processes.

....Elizabeth Traub at Elizabeth Traub Consulting (www.elizabethtraub.com) for "getting us" and helping us spread our message through social media.

...of course, all of our wonderful clients for trusting us, and for having the courage to change their worlds.

CPSIA information can be obtained
at www.ICGtesting.com
Printed in the USA
FSOW04n1331201215
14423FS